Also By Richard O'Connor

Honour: A Historical Golf Novel

Francis Ouimet and the 1913 United States Open

Wooden Bat Baseball Leagues in America

Also By David B. Stinson

Deadball, A Metaphysical Baseball Novel

The United States Court of Federal Claims Handbook and Procedures Manual

Also By Richard O'Connor and David B. Stinson

The Silver Spring-Takoma Thunderbolts - 15th Anniversary Yearbook

THE COLLEGE BASEBALL PRIMER

A GUIDE TO COLLEGE BASEBALL, RECRUITING, SCHOLARSHIPS, AND SUMMER COLLEGIATE WOODEN BAT LEAGUES

THE COLLEGE BASEBALL PRIMER

A GUIDE TO COLLEGE BASEBALL, RECRUITING, SCHOLARSHIPS, AND SUMMER COLLEGIATE WOODEN BAT LEAGUES

RICHARD O'CONNOR

And

DAVID B. STINSON

HUNTINGTON PARK PUBLICATIONS

ISBN-10: 0-98366-892-2
ISBN-13: 978-0-98366-892-3

Published in 2015 by:
Huntington Park Publications, Inc.
8639B 16th Street, Suite 200
Silver Spring, Maryland 20910

www.huntingtonparkpublications.com

PRINTED IN THE UNITED STATES

First Edition, Second Printing

Cover Photograph and Design by David B. Stinson

Cover Layout: Another Stinsongs Production

TABLE OF CONTENTS

CONTENTS

CONTENTS

CONTENTS

INTRODUCTION

Every year approximately 475,000 student-athletes play varsity baseball for their respective high schools. Some 53,000 high school players will play baseball at a college or university. Less than half of that number will receive a baseball scholarship to play for their respective college or university.

The College Baseball Primer offers prospective student-athletes and their parents or guardians a road map to beat the odds and make the college team. *The College Baseball Primer* covers the structure of college baseball, including organization and eligibility, scholarships awards and national letters of intent, how to be seen and get noticed by college recruiters, recruiting guidelines, rules and pointers regarding campus visits and tryouts, agents and non-college staff recruiters, how coaches evaluate potential student-athletes, and noted differences in the various college baseball conferences.

The College Baseball Primer includes a checklist for potential student-athletes beginning with their sophomore year in high school. Once a potential student-athlete beats the odds and makes the team, *The College Baseball Primer* covers issues such as redshirts, transfers, walk-ons, and the Major League Baseball draft. *The College Baseball Primer* also provides information about Summer Collegiate Baseball Leagues, the differences between the leagues, and how to join a team

For the first time anywhere, *The College Baseball Primer* provides a list of every college baseball program organized by conference, including National Collegiate Athletic Association (NCAA) Division I, NCAA Division II, NCAA Division III, the National Association of Intercollegiate Athletics (NAIA), the National Junior College Athletic Association (NJCAA), the Northwest Athletic Association of Community Colleges (NAACC), · the California Community College Athletic Association (CCCAA),

1

the United States Collegiate Athletic Association (USCAA), and the National Christian College Athletic Association (NCCAA).

The search for the right school and program takes patience, hard work, and numerous contacts. *The College Baseball Primer* is a must for anyone who wants to make the team and play college baseball.

CHAPTER 1

A BRIEF HISTORY OF COLLEGE BASEBALL

Four colleges claim to have played the first recorded intercollegiate baseball game. Amherst College and Williams College played on July 1, 1859. The teams used the "Massachusetts Rules" for the game and Amherst won 73 to 32. St. John's College (now known as Fordham University) and St. Francis Xavier (now Xavier High School in New York City) played a game on November 3, 1859, utilizing the "Knickerbocker Rules." St. John's College defeated St. Francis Xavier 33 to 11 in a game that more closely resembled modern-day baseball. As of 2011, Fordham had won more baseball games than any other program in NCAA Division I history.[1]

The first intercollegiate baseball league, known as the Intercollegiate Base Ball Association, was formed in 1879. The fledgling league included Amherst, Brown University, Dartmouth College, and Princeton University. The association prohibited professional players from playing in league games.

The first college conference to play for a conference baseball championship was the Big Ten in 1896, which was won by the University of Chicago. The longest college baseball game was played between the University of Texas and Boston College on May 30, 2009, in a Division I Regional Tournament game at Austin, Texas. Texas defeated Boston three to two in 25 innings. The game lasted seven hours and three minutes. The second longest game in tournament history occurred in a 2012 Regional Round game between the Kent State Golden Flashes and the Kentucky Wildcats

---

[1] New York Times, April 6, 2007, p. D7.

at the U.S. Steel Yard in Gary, Indiana. Kent State beat Kentucky seven to six in 21 innings.

In 1947, the first Division I College Baseball World Series championship was played between the University of California and Yale University. California won the best of three series which included future President George H.W. Bush playing first base for Yale. The first Division II championship was played in 1968, with Chapman University defeating Delta State University. The first Division III championship was played in 1976 when California State University, Stanislaus, defeated Ithaca College. The National Junior College Athletic Association crowned its first national champion in 1958.

The National College Baseball Hall of Fame, located in Lubbock, Texas, was founded in 2006 and is operated by the College Baseball Foundation. The Hall of Fame annually inducts five former collegiate players and five former coaches in addition to two veteran players (from the pre-1947 era). The National College Baseball Hall of Fame inaugural class consisted of five former coaches and five former players and was inducted on July 4, 2006.[2] Every year thereafter, more players and coaches have been enshrined. [3]

Coaches are eligible for induction after the completion of their active collegiate career and must have at least 300 career wins or won at least 65 percent of their coached games. Players are eligible five years after their final collegiate season and must have completed one year of competition at a four-year institution. Players also must have been named to an All-American team (post-1947), an All-League team (pre-1947), or received national prominence. Pre-1947 players and coaches are nominated and voted on by Veteran and Historical Committees. An additional factor considered by the Hall

---

[2] collegebaseballhall.org.
[3] Ibid

of Fame for both players and coaches is good citizenship both during and after their active careers.[4]

Members of the National College Baseball Hall of Fame:

<u>Players</u>

Year	Inductee	University
2006	Will Clark	Mississippi State University
2006	Bob Horner	Arizona State University
2006	Brooks Kieschnick	University of Texas
2006	Dave Winfield	University of Minnesota
2006	Robin Ventura	Oklahoma State University
2007	Jim Abbott	University of Michigan
2007	Pete Incaviglia	Oklahoma State University
2007	Fred Lynn	U. of Southern California
2007	John Olerud	Washington State University
2007	Phil Stephenson	Wichita State University
2007	Derek Tatsuno	University of Hawaii
2008	Steve Arlin	Ohio State University
2008	Eddie Bane	Arizona State University
2008	Floyd Bannister	Arizona State University
2008	Neal Heaton	University of Miami
2008	Burt Hooton	University of Texas
2008	Dick Howser	Florida State University
2008	Ben McDonald	Louisiana State University
2008	Greg Swindell	University of Texas
2009	Joe Carter	Wichita State University
2009	Darren Dreifort	Wichita State University
2009	Kirk Dressendorfer	University of Texas
2009	Barry Larkin	University of Michigan
2009	Keith Moreland	University of Texas
2009	Rafael Palmeiro	Mississippi State University
2009	Todd Walker	Louisiana State University

---

[4] College Baseball Hall of Fame Inductees, collegebaseballhall.org.

Year	Inductee	University
2010	Alan Bannister	Arizona State University
2010	Eddy Furniss	Louisiana State University
2010	Don Heinkel	Wichita State University
2010	Dave Magadan	University of Alabama
2010	B. J. Surhoff	University of North Carolina
2010	Rich Wortham	University of Texas
2011	Terry Francona	University of Arizona
2011	Danny Goodwin	Southern University
2011	Dick Groat	Duke University
2011	Oddibe McDowell	Arizona State University
2011	Tim Wallach	California State U. Fullerton
2012	Lou Brock	Southern University
2012	Nomar Garciaparra	Georgia Tech
2012	Tim Jorgensen	U. of Wisconsin Oshkosh
2012	Brad Wilkerson	University of Florida
2013	Sal Bando	Arizona State University
2013	Tom Borland	Oklahoma State University
2013	Tino Martinez	University of Tampa
2014	Bill Bordley	U. of Southern California
2014	Alex Fernandez	University of Miami
2014	Mike Fiore	University of Miami
2014	Mickey Sullivan	Baylor University

Head Coaches

2006	Skip Bertman	Louisiana State University
2006	Rod Dedeaux	U. of Southern California
2006	Ron Fraser	University of Miami
2006	Cliff Gustafson	University of Texas
2006	Bobby Winkles	Arizona State University
2007	Chuck Brayton	Washington State University
2007	Jim Brock	Arizona State University
2007	Bibb Falk	University of Texas

Year	Inductee	University
2007	Jerry Kindall	University of Arizona
2007	Dick Siebert	University of Minnesota
2008	Bob Todd	Ohio State University
2008	Gary Ward	Oklahoma State University
		New Mexico State University
2009	Gordie Gillespie	University of St. Francis
2009	Ron Polk	Georgia Southern University
		Mississippi State
2010	Bob Bennett	Fresno State
2010	Wally Kincaid	Cerritos College
2011	Bill Wilhelm	Clemson University
2012	Ed Cheff	Lewis–Clark State College
2012	Wayne Graham	San Jacinto College, Rice
2012	Frank Sancet	University of Arizona
2013	Don Schaly	Marietta College
2013	John Winkin	Colby College
2014	Gene Stephenson	Wichita State University
2014	Demie Mainieri	Miami-Dade North

Veterans

Year	Inductee	University
2007	Jack Barry	College of the Holy Cross
2007	Lou Gehrig	Columbia University
2007	Christy Mathewson	Bucknell University
2007	Joe Sewell	University of Alabama
2008	Billy Disch	University of Texas
2008	Owen Carroll	College of the Holy Cross
2008	Jackie Robinson	U. of Southern California
2009	Branch Rickey	Ohio Wesleyan University
		University of Michigan
2010	George Sisler	University of Michigan
2010	Charles Teague	Wake Forest University
2011	Ralph W. E. Jones	Grambling State University

Year	Inductee	University
2012	Frank Suncet	University of Arizona
2013	Ralph Garr	Grambling State University
2014	William C. Matthews	Tuskegee Institute

CHAPTER 2

THE STRUCTURE OF COLLEGE BASEBALL

A.   ORGANIZATION

There are five national governing bodies and two regional organizations that regulate the over 1600 college baseball programs in the United States.

1.   NCAA - National Collegiate Athletic Association (ncaa.org)

Founded in 1906, the NCAA governs 1,085 affiliated college and university baseball programs spread over three divisions: Division I (355 teams, 33 conferences), Division II (288 teams, 26 conferences), and Division III (442 teams, 46 conferences). In 2012, NCAA-affiliated colleges and universities awarded over $1.1 billion in baseball scholarships. See Appendix 1 for a complete listing of NCAA conferences and teams

Each college or university decides which division to join based upon such factors as enrollment, financial awards, and fan support. Some colleges and universities field multiple teams in different divisions (for example, Fairleigh Dickinson University fields two baseball teams, one playing in Division I and one in Division III).

2.   NAIA - National Association of Intercollegiate Athletics (naia.org)

Founded in 1952, the NAIA includes smaller colleges and universities in the United States and Canada. In 2014, 258 NAIA members offered baseball programs spread over two divisions, Division I and Division II.

9

3.   **NJCAA- National Junior College Athletic Association (njcaa.org)**

Founded in 1938, the NJCAA is an association of junior college and community colleges in the United States. In 2014, there were 42 baseball conferences divided into 24 regions. The teams are divided into three divisions: Division I, Division II, and Division III.

4.   **NCCAA - National Christian College Athletic Association (thenccaa.org)**

Founded in 1968 in Canton, Ohio, the NCCAA includes Bible Colleges and small Christian Colleges and Universities in the United States. In 2014 there were 79 baseball programs in the NCCAA. These teams are divided into Division I and Division II..

5.   **CCCAA- California Community College Athletic Association (cccaasports.org)**

The CCCAA includes junior college and community colleges located in California. The Association is divided into 10 conferences and includes 101 CCCAA baseball programs.

6.   **NWAACC- Northwest Athletic Association of Community Colleges (nwaacc.org)**

The NWAACC was founded in 1978 and includes 34 junior and community colleges located in Oregon, Washington, and British Columbia.

7.   **USCAA - United States Collegiate Athletic Association (uscaa.org)**

The USCAA was founded in 2001 and includes 82 member colleges and universities in 24 states.

B.   ELIGIBILITY

1.   **Eligibility Centers**

The NCAA and the NAIA have established separate eligibility centers where student-athletes must register to be eligible to play baseball at one of the member schools. Student-athletes should register with each of these eligibility centers at the beginning of their junior year in high school. Registration can be completed on-line.

a.   **NCAA Eligibility Center**

Registration is required for Division I and Division II colleges and universities only. No registration is needed for Division III programs. Register at eligibilitycenter.org.

b.   **NAIA Eligibility Center**

Registration is required for Division I and Division II colleges and universities. Register at playnaia.org/psaregister.php. A transfer student's eligibility is decided by the individual college or university.

c.   **NJCAA Eligibility Determination**

Each individual college determines an individual student-athlete's eligibility based upon NJCAA Guidelines.

d.   **NJACC, NCCAA, CCCAA, NWAACC, and USCAA**

The NJACC, NCCAA, CCCAA, NWAACC, and USCAA do not conduct eligibility centers.

2.   **Eligibility Requirements**

A student-athlete must meet the following requirements to play baseball at a member college or university.

a.   NCAA Division I

As noted above, prospective student-athletes must register with the NCAA Eligibility Center (formally the NCAA Eligibility Clearinghouse) and be cleared to participate in college sports. College and university sports programs are unable to offer Division I recruits athletic scholarships unless they have registered first with the NCAA Eligibility Center. Student-athletes must register even if the student-athlete is not seeking a scholarship. To be eligible to receive a scholarship to play for a Division I program, the prospective student-athlete must meet the following requirements.

    i.   Graduate from an accredited high school.

    ii.   Meet core course requirements. For college-bound student-athletes to compete their freshman year, Division I programs requires college-bound student-athletes to complete 16 core courses. Ten of these core courses must be completed by start of the student-athlete's senior year. See Appendix 2 for a complete list of core courses.

    iii.   Meet minimum test scores. Division I utilizes a sliding scale to match test scores and core course grade point averages (GPA). For students enrolling prior to August 1, 2016, the sliding scale outlined in Appendix 3 is applicable. After August 1, 2016, to receive athletic financial aid and to practice with the team, a GPA of 2.0 is required. For competition, the GPA requirement increases to 2.3 in the core courses.

b.   NCAA Division II

To be eligible to receive a scholarship to play for a Division II program, the prospective student-athlete must:

    i .   Graduate from an accredited high school;

    ii.   Complete 16 core courses (See Appendix 2 for a list of core courses);

iii.   Attain at least a 2.0 GPA in core courses;

iv.   Obtain a combined 820 on the SAT or 18 on ACT.

If a student-athlete does not meet all of the academic requirements listed above, the student-athlete can become a partial qualifier at a Division II program by meeting one of the following standards:

i.   Combine SAT score of 820 or ACT score of 18;

ii.   Completion of 16 core courses with a 2.0 GPA.

A student athlete who is a partial qualifier may:

i.   Practice with the team during the first year of college;

ii.   Receive financial aid the first year;

iii.   Play four seasons;

iv.   Not compete during the academic first year.

c.   **NCAA Division III**

Each college or university sets its own standards for admittance. To be eligible for competition, a player must be enrolled in at least 12 semester hours of classes working toward a baccalaureate degree or the equivalent. No Division III student-athlete may receive an athletic scholarship. Each student-athlete must meet the NCAA standard for amateurism to play baseball.

The NCAA amateur rules prohibit a student-athlete from (i) having contacts with professional teams, (ii) receiving a salary to play baseball, (iii) playing baseball with professional players, (iv) trying out with a professional team, (v) being represented by an agent, and (vi) receiving benefits from an agent. Each student-athlete who registers with the NCAA Eligibility Center is required to complete a questionnaire on their amateur status which is utilized by the member program to determine the eligibility of the student-athlete to play for their team.

d.   **NAIA Baseball**

To be eligible to receive a scholarship to play for a NAIA member program, a prospective student-athlete must graduate from high school, as well as meet two out of three of the following requirements:

i.   Obtain a score of 18 on the ACT or 860 on the SAT;

ii.   Maintain a 2.0 GPA in core courses;

iii.   Graduate in the top one half of their high school class.

e.   **NJCAA**

To be eligible to receive a scholarship to play at a NJCAA member program, a prospective student-athlete must either graduate from high school and receive a diploma, or hold a General Education Degree (GED).

f.   **NCCAA**

To be eligible to receive a scholarship to play at a NCCAA member program, a prospective student-athlete must graduate from an accredited high school in the upper half of the graduating class and meet at least one of the following criteria:

i.   Obtain a minimum score of 18 on the enhanced ACT or 860 on the SAT;

ii.   Have a minimum overall high school grade point average of 2.0 on 4.0 scale.

Prior to enrolling, the prospective student-athlete must fill out an NCCAA Eligibility Certificate, which then is filed with the NCCAA prior to the student athlete participating in the sport.

g.   **CCCAA**

To be eligible to receive a scholarship to play at a CCCAA member program, a prospective student-athlete must graduate from an accredited high school.

h.   **NWAACC Baseball**

To be eligible to receive a scholarship to play at a NWAACC member program, a prospective student-athlete must graduate from a high school and maintain a cumulative GPA of 2.0 during any semester while enrolled.

CHAPTER 3

SCHOLARSHIPS

College baseball is deemed an equivalency sport, meaning that scholarship offers can be divided into a multitude of shares. A player can receive from a 25 percent scholarship, up to a full scholarship, which may include college tuition, fees, room and board, and course-related books for one year. Scholarships are one year grants which may or may not be renewed. An analysis of baseball scholarships in 2012 found that Division I program scholarships fell into the following range:

Pitchers typically receive 50 to 60 percent scholarships, with less than ten percent of such players receiving full scholarships.

Middle infielders typically receive 40 to 60 percent scholarships, with less than five percent of such players receiving full scholarships.

Corner infielders and outfielders typically receive 33 to 40 percent scholarships, with less than five percent of such players receiving full scholarships.[5]

A.   SCHOLARSHIP AWARDS

1.   **NCAA Division I**

Division I programs are allowed 11.7 scholarships per year. Division I baseball programs once were allowed 13 scholarships, prior to a 10 percent cut in 1991, which reduced the number to 11.7. A total of 27 players may receive scholarships, with the minimum scholarship being 25 percent. The maximum number of players on a

---

[5] WPIAL Baseball Coaches Association, wpabaseball.com.

Division I roster is 35. Division I programs can provide a student-athlete assistance with tuition, fees, room and board, and course-related books.

2.   **NCAA Division II**

Division II programs can offer nine scholarships each year. Division II schools also can provide a student-athlete assistance with tuition, fees, room and board, and course-related books.

3.   **NCAA Division III**

Division III programs do not offer any athletic scholarships, but can offer merit-based scholarships, need-based scholarships, or financial aid to eligible students who play baseball.

4.   **NJCAA**

NJCAA programs offer up to 24 scholarships per year. Some Division I NJCAA programs offer full scholarships, but most offer partial scholarships.

Division II NJCAA programs may award only funding for tuition, fees, and course-related books. Division III NJCAA programs do not award any funding to student-athletes.

5.   **NAIA**

NAIA Division I and II programs offer up to 12 full scholarships per year. Division III programs do not offer scholarships.

Few NAIA programs offer full scholarships to student-athletes. Partial scholarships are more common. To receive scholarship funding and to play on a team, a student-athlete must be enrolled in at least 12 credit hours.

6.   **NCCAA**

NCCAA baseball programs can offer up to 12 scholarships per year. Scholarships are available only in Division I programs.

7.   **CCCAA**

CCCAA baseball programs can offer up to 11 scholarships per year.

8.   **NWAACC**

NWAACC baseball programs can offer up to 11 scholarships per year.

9.   **USCAA**

USCAA baseball programs can offer up to nine scholarships per year.

B.   NATIONAL LETTER OF INTENT

The National Letter of Intent (NLI) is a binding contract between the student-athlete and the college or university. If the student-athlete signs a NLI, the student-athlete agrees to attend the college or university for at least one year (two semesters) and the college or university agrees to provide the student-athlete with a scholarship. The deadlines to sign a NLI can change yearly, but typically are the second week of November (Early Period) or early April to early August (Regular Period), both in the year prior to the student-athlete's entering the college or university. Once a NLI is signed, the student-athlete is prohibited from negotiating with another college or university.

Under no circumstance should a student-athlete sign more than one NLI. If a student-athlete breaches the terms of the NLI by attending another college or university, the student-athlete will lose one year of eligibility for that college or university (meaning the student-athlete will have only three years of eligibility instead of four).

A NLI should be accompanied by a financial aid agreement from the college or university. The financial aid agreement is a one year contract which can be renewed for up to three more years. If the college or university has not provided a financial aid agreement, the student-athlete should not sign a NLI. Also, a student-athlete does not need to sign a NLI in order to receive financial aid. A NLI and a financial aid agreement are two separate documents.

A NCAA college or university coach cannot be present when the student-athlete signs the NLI.

CHAPTER 4

How To Be Seen And Get Noticed By College Recruiters

There are a variety of methods by which prospective student-athletes can gain the attention of college recruiters. The suggestions discussed below are intended for individuals who are not already recognized as being in the Top 100 of high school players in the country (student-athletes in this top category already have gained notice of college scouts). For those individuals who make up the other 99.9 percent, a persistent and aggressive approach is necessary to get noticed by college recruiters.

A.   CAMPS AND SHOWCASES

1.   **College Sponsored Camps**. In 2013, there were 79 Division I sponsored baseball camps run by Division I coaches for players ranging from the ages of 15 to 18. These camps are an excellent opportunity for high school players to be seen by specific college coaches and to develop early on a relationship with the coaching staff of specific college teams. Division II and NJCAA programs also offer camps throughout the year. A list of camps is available at www.collegebaseballcamps.com.

2.   **Showcases**. There are hundreds of high school showcases held throughout the country each year. Interested student-athletes should check the experience level of the group sponsoring the showcase, including the number of years the organization has run showcases and the success rate of the showcases in placing players in collegiate programs. It is important to determine not only the number of college recruiters who are committed to attend the showcase, but how many have actually

registered. Showcases worth attending will publish beforehand a list of colleges and coaches attending the showcase.

There is a difference between true recruiting showcases and camps that simply develop players for future showcases (check the age level of those invited to attend). A good showcase should offer repetitive skill drills, instruction of fundamentals, and a written evaluation after completing the showcase. Local scouts, high school coaches, and travel coaches all should be familiar with local showcases and should be able to offer recommendations to potential student-athletes.

3.   **What Can College Coaches Do And Not Do At Camps/Showcases**. Pursuant to NCAA rules, if a showcase or a camp is offered during a quiet period, no college coaches can be present at the showcase or camp (see Chapter 5, Section A). A college coach is prohibited from speaking with potential student-athletes at a showcase or camp until after July 1st for student-athletes who have reached their junior year in high school.

B.   CONTACTING COLLEGE COACHES

College coaches are restricted on when and how they can contact potential recruits. However, potential student-athletes are not restricted on how or when they can contact a college coach. It is important nonetheless for potential student-athletes to show restraint and be selective in who is contacted and how. For many college coaches, the number one irritation in recruiting is receiving a deluge of mailings from a recruit, either through email or direct mail. The following are suggestions on how to show proper restraint when contacting a college coach:

1.   **Be Professional**. Any contact, either through email or direct mail, should be well written, concise, and contain no grammatical errors. It is best to have a second set of eyes review all recruiting correspondence prior sending it out. Correspondence should be directed to the appropriate college staff member

responsible for recruiting. Research the college team through its website or athletic directory (high school coaches also should be able to find this information if it is not available on line) and determine the person is at the college whose job it is to recruit baseball players. If the information still isn't readily available, contact directly the college or university athletic department.

2.　　**Recruiting Questionnaire**. Many colleges utilize a recruiting questionnaire which typically is available online from the college or university website. The form will be entitled "Prospect Athlete Form," "Recruit Questionnaire," "Information on Candidate," or something similar. Great care should be taken to respond to all questions on the form. Questionnaires should be submitted to the college or university during the prospective student-athlete's junior year in high school. During the first semester of their senior year, prospective student-athletes should follow up with an email to each program to whom a questionnaire was sent, stating the student-athlete's continued interest in the program and providing updated information or statistics from the previous season.

3.　　**Recruiting Video/Web Site**. The internet offers excellent opportunities for self promotion by prospective student-athletes. Again, restraint and proper editing are keys to effective promotion. An effective video should last no longer than two to three minutes. Videos should be structured as follows:

To demonstrate skills, take a video of the player showcasing his talent.

To demonstrate hitting, the video should include the player from various angles, both in batting practice and in game footage.

College coaches and professional scouts are not looking for players who still need to be taught basic skills, so player videos should demonstrate proper mechanics and footwork.

Outfielders should demonstrate their longest accurate throws after catching fly balls and after fielding ground balls.

Infielders should demonstrate ideal footwork getting to and going through the throws across the diamond.

Pitchers should demonstrate the types of pitches they can throw, along with a speed gun reading indicating the speed of the pitches. Coaches also like to see if the pitcher can throw from the stretch. Slide-steps and pick-offs are bonuses if players can showcase them to their benefit.

Catchers should demonstrate their blocking skills, receiving skills, and footwork when blocking and retrieving. Release times and footwork to second base and to third base are also recommended. When filming the video, catchers are encouraged to have a still player in the batter's box from the right side to showcase ability to work around the batter.

A player needs to showcase the player's best attributes. If a player's best attribute is size, include footage showing the players size and strength.

All position players should run the 60-yard dash and know their time. If a player's best attribute is speed, include footage of the player running the 60 yard dash, running from home to first base, and stealing a base. If speed is not an attribute, do not include in the video the player running a 60 yard dash.

If a player's best attribute is hitting, include footage from the vantage point of the catcher of where the ball travels once hit.

If a player's best attribute is defensive fielding, for infielders, include footage of more defense (double plays, plays in the hole, charging, routine, and backhand).

For outfielders, include footage of the player throwing from the outfield to home or third base, taken from the vantage point of the second baseman or shortstop.

If a player's best attribute is arm strength, include footage of where the player throws to and where the ball ends up. The video should be taken from the vantage point of the catcher for outfielders and first base for infielders.

If arm strength is not an attribute, zoom in on footwork and release. For outfielders, show approach for grounders and fly balls (getting behind ball, and staying down and through on grounders).

Ending. Close the video with a statement on why you want to attend the particular school and how you believe you can contribute to the baseball program. The best videos provide a complete picture of a player without coming across as cocky or exceedingly boisterous.

In order to keep down the cost of such videos, consider asking a fellow student (someone who is studying film production) to shoot and edit the video. Once the video is finished, send it directly to the person in charge of recruiting at the college or university and include with it a letter of introduction. The video also can be posted online (for example, on youtube.com).

4.   **Walk-Ons**. Players who have graduated from high school but have not yet been selected by their college team have the option to try out for that team as a walk-on. College and university teams often hold walk-on opportunities, typically in early September. Information about walk-on tryouts should be available on the college or university website or by contacting the coaching staff member in charge of recruitment.

5.   **High School Coach Recommendations**. High school coaches can be an effective resource for prospective student-athletes by providing referrals to college and university coaches. Ideally, high school coach recommendations should be sent to college and university coaches during the early fall of the prospective student-athlete's senior year.

CHAPTER 5

RECRUITING

A.   RECRUITING GUIDLINES

There are limitations on how and when college and university coaches and staff may recruit prospective student-athletes. These restrictions vary according to the league and the division in which the college or university participates.

1.   **NCAA Division I**

The NCAA has identified three different types of periods relevant to recruiting by colleges and universities: contact period, quiet period, and dead period.

Contact Period. A college or university coach may make in-person contact with potential student-athletes or their parents either on or off the campus of the college or university, or in writing or over the phone. A coach also may visit high schools to watch the potential student-athlete play. Potential student-athletes and their parents may visit the campus of any college or university.

Dead Period. A college or university coach may not have any in-person contact with potential student-athletes or their parents either on or off campus. However, college coaches may write and call potential student-athletes or their parents.

Quiet Period. A college or university coach may not make any in-person contact with potential student-athletes or their parents off the campus of the college or university. A college coach may not watch potential student-athletes play or visit their high schools. A college coach may write or call potential student-athletes or their parents. Potential student-athletes may visit the campus of the college or university.

Recruiting Calendar. The dates in the calendar set forth below reflect the application of Division I Bylaw 13.17.1 at the time of publication of this manual. They are subject to change per NCAA Constitution 5.2.3.1 or if certain dates (e.g., National Letter of Intent signing dates) are altered. Recruiting calendar dates change often so be sure to check for any updated calendar dates.

August 1 to 31 (Contact Period)

September 1 to 13 (Quiet Period)

September 14 to November 11 (Contact Period)

November 12 to 15 (Dead Period)

November 16 to January 2 (Quiet Period)

January 3 to January 7 (Dead Period)

January 8 to February 28 (Quiet Period)

March 1 to July 31 (Contact Period)

Recruiting Material. Recruiters are forbidden from sending recruitment materials to potential student-athletes before September 1st of the potential student-athlete's junior year of high school.

Telephone/In Person Recruitment. In-person recruitment is not allowed until July 1st after completion of the potential student-athlete's junior year. This rule also applies to contact with relatives of students-athletes. However, colleges and universities are allowed to invite players to participate in sports camps on campus prior to September 1st of the student-athlete's junior year. Student-athletes are allowed to call or visit colleges and universities on their own. College and university coaches may attend camps and tournaments to observe players (except during a Quiet Period), but they may not speak with specific players.

Official Visits. During a student-athlete's senior year in high school a student-athlete may make five official campus visits that are paid for by colleges or universities. Coaches are allowed one telephone call contact per week after a campus visit.

Signing Period. Once the student-athlete is committed to a college or university, the player may sign a letter of intent during one of several specific signing periods. Signing period deadlines can change yearly. Currently, the early signing period for a Division I baseball player is between November 8 and 15; the late signing period is April 11 to August 13.

2. **NCAA Division II**

Recruiting Materials. Recruiters are forbidden from sending recruitment materials to potential student-athletes before June 15th of potential student-athlete's senior year in high school.

Telephone Contact. College or university coaches may call a student-athlete (after June 15th of their junior year) once per week.

Email Contact. If a student-athlete emails a college or university coach, the coach can respond via email at any time.

Official Visits. Student-athletes can make up to five official visits, which are limited to one official visit per college.

Unofficial Visits. A student-athlete can make an unlimited number of unofficial visits to colleges or universities.

3. **NCAA Division III**

Recruiting Materials. Potential student-athletes may receive printed materials from coaches and their respective colleges and universities at any time.

Telephone Calls. College and university coaches may make telephone contact at any time. Potential student-athletes are likewise free to contact college and university coaches.

Written Contact. College and university coaches may send recruiting materials to prospective student-athletes at any time.

Off Campus Contact. College and university coaches may make off campus contact with student-athletes after the student-athlete's junior year in high school.

Campus Visits. Potential student-athletes may make unlimited unofficial visits to the campus of any college or university. Official campus visits paid for by the college or university are allowed after the first day of high school classes of the potential student-athlete's senior year. However, a student athlete may make only one official visit to the college or university.

Off Campus Evaluation. There are no restrictions on the number of contacts and evaluations that may be made by coaches or potential student-athletes.

4.   **NJCAA**

Telephone Recruiting. There are no restrictions on junior college coaches contacting or speaking with potential players.

Recruitment Calendar. There is no formal recruitment calendar. Junior college coaches have no limits on their contact with high school players from freshmen to junior year. During a player's senior year the same rules apply unless the high school player already has enrolled in another institution (e.g., the high school senior has enrolled in a college to take introductory classes during senior year). If that is the case, no contact by the junior college coach is allowed.

Campus Visits. An institution may pay for one visit to the campus, not to exceed two days and two nights. The visit must be completed no less than 10 days prior to the opening day of classes.

High School Tryouts/Showcases. These are allowed as long as authorized by the State High School Activities Association regulations in the student-athlete's home state

5. **NAIA**

Recruitment Calendar. There is no formal recruitment calendar. NAIA coaches have no limits on their contact with high school players from freshmen to junior year. During a player's senior year the same rules apply unless the high school player already has enrolled in another institution.

Campus Visits. A NAIA institution may pay for one campus visit for a stay not to exceed two days and two nights. The visit must be completed no less than ten days prior to the opening day of classes.

6. **NCCAA**

The NCCAA has not adopted any contact rules.

7. **CCCAA**

Telephone Contact. There are no limits on such contacts by a coach with a student-athlete.

Recruiting Material. There is no limit on the amount of material or when it can be sent.

Official Visits. College or university may pay for travel expenses for a visit if inside California. No rules on paying for housing during visit.

Unofficial Visits. There is no restriction on unofficial visits.

8. **NWAACC**

Telephone Contact. The following states limit coach telephone contact with student-athletes to only their senior year:

Washington, Oregon, Alaska, British Columbia, Idaho, Montana, Nevada and Hawaii.

Recruiting Material. The following states limit material sent by coaches to student-athletes to only their senior year: Washington, Oregon, Alaska, British Columbia, Idaho, Montana, Nevada and Hawaii.

Official Visits. Schools can pay for student-athletes lodging and meals if the student-athlete comes from within recruiting area.

Transportation Expenses Excluded. No state funds can be used to pay student-athlete transportation costs. Colleges must use contributed funds for these expenses.

Unofficial Visits. No restrictions.

9.   **USCCAA**

There are no rules regarding telephone contacts, recruiting material, official and unofficial visits. Most member programs follow the NAIA Rules on contact.

B.   CAMPUS VISITS AND TRYOUTS FOR PROSPECTIVE STUDENT-ATHLETES

The NAIA approach toward campus visits by prospective student-athletes, as summarized below by Game Ready Scout Day, is based on the following principles:

1.   The protection of the student-athlete in maintaining normal academic progress in high school and junior college.

2.   The coordination of this rule with the overall policies of the institution affecting procurement of student-athletes with special talents.

3.   The control of tryouts consistent with making the intercollegiate program an integral part of the total program without legislating against the student-athlete.

4.   Campus visits and tryouts may take place under the following conditions.

a.   Individual or group tryouts may be conducted, on the member institution's campus only, for the purpose of assessing athletic promise if tryouts are a part of the general institutional policy in the evaluation and admission of students with special talents. Tryouts, where permitted, shall be limited to no more than two days for a specific student at a member institution.

b.   No part of the travel expense, meals, and lodging of prospective student-athletes making visitations to an institution shall be paid by the institution unless such practice is a part of the general institutional policy in procurement of other students with special talents and not only for the express purpose of securing athletes.

c.   Visitation of prospective student-athletes shall not involve loss of school time, except where such visitation occurs as a part of the total visitation program of the institution, approved by the administration of both the host institution and the institution of the visiting prospective student.[6]

C.   AGENTS AND NON-COLLEGE STAFF RECRUITERS

1.   **NCAA Division I**

a.   NCAA Bylaw 12.3

A student-athlete (any individual who currently participates in or who may be eligible in the future to participate in intercollegiate sport) may not agree verbally or in writing to be represented by an

---

[6] Gamereadyscoutday.com.

athlete agent in the present or in the future for the purpose of marketing the student-athlete's ability or reputation. If the student-athlete enters into such an agreement, the student-athlete is ineligible for intercollegiate competition. Also, a student-athlete may not accept transportation or other benefits from an athlete agent. This prohibition also applies to the student-athlete's relatives and friends.[7]

b. Agents

The term "agent" includes actual agents, runners (individuals who befriend student-athletes and frequently distribute impermissible benefits), and financial advisors. It is not a violation of NCAA rules if a student-athlete merely talks to an agent (as long as an agreement for agent representation is not established) or socializes with an agent. For example, a student-athlete could go to dinner with an agent and no NCAA violations would occur. (NCAA Guidance Memo, July 29, 2010).

c. Advisors

Student-athletes can seek advice from parents, former coaches, so-called advisors (providing NCAA rules are not violated), and attorneys. Attorneys, however, may not have any contact with a professional sports team to discuss a contract offer.

d. College and University Panels

The NCAA permits colleges and universities to form Professional Sports Counseling Panels to assist student-athletes. These panels may review proposed contracts, provide advice concerning the purchase of disability insurance, meet with representatives from professional teams, and assist the student-athlete in the selection of an agent.[8]

---

[7] NCAA Bylaw 12.3.1.
[8] NCAA Bylaw 12.3.1-12.3.3.1.

<u>Examples of Players Who Ran Afoul of NCAA</u>
<u>Agent/Advisor Rule</u>:

Albert Minnis, a pitcher from Lawrence High School, was chosen by the Atlanta Braves in the 33rd round of 2010 draft. He decided to attend Wichita State and enlisted the services of an unpaid adviser to determine his pro potential. The unpaid advisor contacted the Atlanta Braves staff subsequent to when Minnis had enrolled at Wichita State. The NCAA found this to be a violation and suspended Minnis for 30 games.[9]

Logan Ehlers, a pitcher at the University of Nebraska was suspended for 60 percent of the 2011 season because his advisor had a "30-second contact" with staff from the Toronto Blue Jays during the 2011 Cape Cod summer league season.[10]

2.   **NCAA Division II and III**

Both NCAA Divisions II and III programs follow the same Agent/Advisor rules as Division I programs.

3.   **NAIA and NJCAA**

Both NAIA and NJCAA member schools do not have specific agent contract rules other than the general prohibition that once a student-athelete signs with an agent, the student-athlete is ineligible to play baseball for a college or university.

---

[9] www.foxnews.com/sports/2011/04/06/college-baseball-reconsiders-murky-rule-agents/#ixzz2GwxY3hq1.

[10] www.foxnews.com/sports/2011/04/06/college-baseball-reconsiders-murky-rule-agents/#ixzz2Gwz9yez0.

D.   AN AGENT/ADVISOR'S PERSPECTIVE[11]

The rule in college baseball is that a prospective student-athlete shall be ineligible to participate in an intercollegiate sport if the student-athlete orally or in writing had been represented by an agent for the purpose of marketing the student-athlete's abilities in a specific sport. In 2012, the NCAA adopted a new rule: "securing advice from a lawyer concerning a proposed sports contract shall not be considered contracting for representation under this rule."[12] Five other governing bodies (NAIA, NJCAA, NCCAA, CCCAA and NWCAC) subsequently adopted the same rule.

Warning to Student-Athlete: If you tell anyone you are represented by an agent, you immediately become ineligible to play college baseball.

As a result of this new rule, the term "advisor" came into existence. This is especially unique to baseball because, unlike other sports, a player is not required to declare eligibility for the draft. A prospective student-athlete may be approached by a "runner," a person who works for an agency who makes the initial contact with the player. The advisor may be a former player or someone who has some contacts in the baseball industry and has access to players. Because there is so much money to be made in the draft, the number of advisors has increased dramatically in the past few years. An advisor does not need to be a lawyer. Indeed, there are no qualifications to be an advisor. As such, there are many people

---

[11] David Pasti, Certified Major League Baseball Agent. Mr. Pasti represents both major and minor league players and has served as an advisor to college and high school players in the annual baseball draft. Mr. Pasti also is a partner in the Rockville, Maryland, law firm of Shure, Perez, O'Connor, and Pasti, where he focuses on sports management as well as criminal and civil litigation.

[12] NCAA Bylaws 12.3.2

willing to assist potential student-athletes for a fee, some more qualified than others. A prospective student-athlete should seek advice from a lawyer regarding a proposed contract, rather than from a non-regulated runner.

Not every student-athlete needs an advisor. Generally, a potential student-athlete can benefit from an advisor if the student-athlete has been approached by Major League teams. An advisor can assist by explaining the draft process and, more importantly, assist in crafting a response to a team's request for information. For example, a major league team particularly is interested in determining whether a potential student-athlete is willing to sign a contract with the team if drafted. The team will not use a draft pick unless the team believes the potential student-athlete is "signable." Of course, "signability" is a relative term. One person may be signable even though that person wants $500,000, while another person may be unsignable even though that person wants only $50,000. One of the roles of the advisor is to determine the value of the potential student-athlete and help determine whether the student-athlete is willing to be drafted. If a student-athlete is willing to be drafted, the agent will assist in conveying to major league teams a figure that doesn't exceed the student-athlete's value. Teams rarely will draft a potential student-athlete unless they know the student-athlete's "signability" before the draft.

Major League baseball has implemented new rules that penalize a team for exceeding a team's allotted draft amount, thereby putting some constraints on a team's willingness to go over "slot" to sign a player. Each pick in the first five rounds has an amount assigned to it, and an allotted total amount for each team, depending on their position in the draft. This has created some interesting scenarios for college seniors who typically were given only a $1,000 bonus to sign. Now, teams are drafting college seniors earlier in the draft and giving them a lower bonus than the slot, and using that extra money for another pick. It provides some college seniors a reason to have an advisor as they may be contacted during the draft and asked if they would take a certain amount to be drafted. The college senior needs to know how to respond. There is no specific rule that restricts a potential student-athlete from signing a contract with an advisor, although it has been ingrained into most student-athletes that they should never sign anything. Most advisors don't have the players sign any type of agreement. The advisors fee typically is a percentage of the signing bonus, usually three to five percent.

E.   QUESTIONS TO ASK A POTENTIAL AGENT

1.   Are you registered with a state?

2.   Did you graduate from law school? If so, what is the name of school?

3.   What is your professional background and training?

4.   What services do you offer to your clients other than contract negotiations (e.g., financial planning)?

5.   Can you provide a list of current clients?

6.   How do you advance the careers of clients off the field?

7.   Can you provide a sample client fee statement.

8.   What is your fee structure? Are fees negotiable?

9.   Are you bonded (important if agent will be handling your money)?

10.   What is the duration of the agreement?

11.   How will you maximize a free agent client's chances of making a team?

F.   CRITERIA FOR DETERMINING HOW COACHES
     AND SCOUTS EVALUATE PLAYERS.

1.   **Fielding and Hitting**

The process most widely used by college and university
coaches and recruiters (as well as professional scouts) to evaluate
players is the five tool method of evaluation. These five tools also are
used in determining the level of play for college divisions.

The traditional five tool method utilizes a scale of 20 - 80 in
evaluating various aspects of a player's potential. Grades are
provided for each "tool." The grading scale escalates from a low of
20 to a high of 80.

80 = Excellent

70 = Very good

60 = Good

50 = Average

40 = Below average

30 = Well below average

20 = Poor

The five tools include the following:

a.   Hitting. Evaluation of the player's bat speed and
compactness of swing, hand-eye coordination, mechanics, and bat
strength.

b.   Power. Evaluation of the player's ability to drive the
ball. A player with "5 o'clock power" means the player can hit a lot
of balls out in batting practice. Power is usually the last thing to
develop for a hitter.

39

c.   Fielding. Evaluation of the player's hand work, footwork, body control, double play pivot skills, quickness, reaction time, and mental acumen. Catchers are evaluated based on their plate blocking skills, "pop times" (seconds from ball in catcher's mitt to ball in second baseman's glove), handling pitchers, game calling skills, and control.

d.   Throwing. Evaluation of the player's arm strength, length of throw, release, accuracy, and arm speed.

e.   Speed: Evaluation of the time it takes a player to get from home to first. A times of less than four seconds is considered excellent and would obtain a high score (70 - 80).

The five tools may rank differently depending upon which skills are most important to the position of the player being evaluated. Examples include:

Catcher - fielding, throwing, hitting, power, speed

Shortstop- fielding, throwing, hitting, speed, power

Outfielder- hitting, power, throwing, fielding, speed

2.   **Pitcher Evaluations**

Pitchers are graded utilizing the following criteria:

a.   Fastball Velocity. Left handed pitchers typically are expected to throw one or two mph slower than right hand pitchers. Grades vary from 98 MPH+(80) to 85-87 (40).

b.   Additional Factors. Evaluators examine a pitcher's arm speed, balance, consistency of each pitch, movement of pitches, overall mechanics, and velocity.

3.   **Other Factors**

Other Factors used by college and university coaches in evaluating a player include height and weight (and overall physical fitness), travel team experience, academic record, class load (Honors and AP courses), SAT/ACT scores, and GPA.

G.   DIFFERENCES IN NCAA COLLEGE BASEBALL DIVISIONS

1.   **NCAA Division I**

Pitchers typically throw between 88 and 90 mph. Position players typically have at least four of the five measurable tools.

2.   **NCAA Division II**

The average Division II pitcher throws between 83 and 85 mph. Position players may have potential to meet most of the five measurable tools, but require more practice and guidance before they can play at a higher level.

3.   **NCAA Division III**

Pitchers typically throw between 79 and 81 mph.

CHAPTER 6

CHECKLIST FOR PARENTS AND STUDENTS

The search for the right school can be a daunting task and, quite frankly, overwhelming. The key to successful college recruitment is persistence: asking coaches, advisors, and school counselors as many questions as necessary to get the information needed. In this section we provide a recruitment blueprint for potential student-athletes, laying out questions that should be asked along the way.

A.   LATE SOPHOMORE/EARLY JUNIOR YEAR

1.   **Realistic Evaluation**. One of the most important first steps is to have an independent evaluation of the potential student-athlete's skill level. By sophomore year in high school, the player should obtain an evaluation from the following individuals:

a.   <u>High School Coach</u>

Ask the coach to provide an honest, detailed evaluation. This evaluation can be used to develop a work plan on improving certain aspects of the player's skills.

b.   <u>Professional Evaluation</u>

Arrange for a professional skills evaluation of the student-athlete from a local scout, a former college player, or a former professional player. Expect to pay for a professional evaluation. It is worth the cost so that the student-athlete has a realistic understanding of his skills, and what he must do to improve.

The goal at this point is to have in hand by the start of a player's junior year in high school a realistic understanding of the player's strengths and weaknesses, and what must be done to improve.

2.   Research Colleges And Universities

Research colleges and universities to determine ones that best fit the skill level of the potential student-athlete. See Appendix 1 for a complete list of colleges and universities by organization and division, and their respective websites. Focus first on colleges and universities within a 200 mile radius of home to see if any are of interest.

The goal at this point is to identify 10 to 15 colleges or universities. Consult with high school coaches, friends, and academic counselors for their input on possible colleges and universities.

3.   Get Organized

Establish a written or digital folder for each college or university selected and include in that folder:

a.   Name of college or university, division, and conference.

b.   Name of the baseball contact, head coach, and contact information.

c.   A copy of the current team roster with notations on where the players are from (local/national). This information will help gauge whether the college or university recruits from a local pool of applicants or nationally. Potential student-athletes should note the breakdown of players by position so they can determine how many positions are available, not only team wide, but by year (freshmen, sophomores, juniors, seniors). This information also will be useful when meeting with the college or university coach to discuss where a potential student-athlete may fit within the organization.

d.   A copy of the fall and spring baseball schedules with notations on how much travel is required (which obviously will impact studies), and how many games are played (inter-squad, exhibition, and regular season). Some college or universities play upwards of 100 games per year. Potential student-athletes should evaluate the time commitment and decide how much they are willing to devote to baseball.

e.   A copy of the team's record over the past few seasons to evaluate the success of the program.

f.   A list of the cost of attending the college or university, including room and board, tuition, types of scholarships offered, distance from home (for purposes of travel costs), and types of academic programs offered at the college or university.

The goal at this point is to use the research to refine and finalize a list of colleges or universities.

4.   **Academic Advisor**

Meet with the high school academic advisor to discuss the colleges or universities identified, seeking input from the advisor regarding admission and application requirements. The goal at this point is to put together an application plan that meets the requirements and deadlines of the colleges or universities.

5.   **College Visits**

Begin taking unofficial visits of colleges or universities on the list. Tour the campus, dorms, academic buildings, and visit the athletic facilities. Talk with current players about the program. Bring a notebook on any campus visit to record what you learn about the college or university and the baseball program.

After visiting a few colleges and universities, the myriad of information on each program can seem overwhelming, so it is important to keep detailed notes to help keep everything straight. Prior to any college or university visit, be sure to review Chapter 5 for information on restrictions placed on coaches, such as when they may interact with potential student-athletes.

The goal is to visit at least three to five colleges or universities by the end of summer sophomore year.

B. JUNIOR ACADEMIC AND PLAYING YEAR

1. Academic Program

It is important for student-athletes to do well in school to make sure that they meet the recruitment requirements in core courses and GPA. The SAT or ACT exams should be taken no later than the spring of the student-athlete's junior year.

2. Register With The Two Eligibility Centers

Potential student-athletes should register as early as possible with the two eligibility centers in order to put colleges and universities on notice that they are interested in playing collegiate baseball (See Chapter 2, Section B). Student-athletes should ask their high school guidance counselors to send a copy of their transcript to the eligibility centers at the end of their junior year. Where a student-athlete has attended more than one high school, a transcript from each high school must be sent to the eligibility centers. Student-athletes also should complete their amateurism questionnaire provided by the eligibility centers.

3. Skills CD/Video

For description of how to prepare a skills video, see Chapter 4, Section B. Skills videos should be sent to coaches by the end of the potential student-athlete's junior year.

4.   **Questionnaire**

Most college and universities have a questionnaire that potential student-athletes are asked to fill out. Typically these questionnaires seek basic information about a student-athlete's skills and academic record. Care should be taken in completing these questionnaires, using proper grammar and correct spelling, as they typically are the first contact potential student-athletes have with college or university coaches.

5.   **Contact Coaches**

If a potential student-athlete already has identified a college or university program of interest, contact with the coach may be made. However, see section C below about how to go about contacting a college coach.

6.   **College Visits**.

Student-athletes should strive to make an additional three to five unofficial college or university visits.

C.   SENIOR ACADEMIC AND PLAYING YEAR

1.   **Contact Coaches**

Potential student-athletes should send letters (or follow-up letters) to college and university coaches indicating that they are interested in their programs. The letter should include an attachment with the player's most recent baseball statistics. Potential student-athletes may send an unlimited number of letters and emails to coaches, but Division I and Division II coaches are restricted on how and when they can respond. (See Chapter 5). Letters should be sent to the coach's office and not the coach's home.

Although student-athletes have no restrictions in contacting college and university coaches, sending too many letters or emails to the same coach or program may be detrimental to the student-athlete's efforts. A good rule of thumb is to send no more than three emails or letters before the start of senior year. The best time to contact coaches is late September and early October. Coaches are actively recruiting during this time period.

2.   Academic Items

Student-athletes should take the SAT/ACT in their junior year or at the latest, the fall of their senior year. Student-athletes should insure transcripts have been received by the eligibility centers.

3.   Official Visits

Visits should be scheduled in September or October for up to five schools to meet with coaches and learn more about their programs. Campus visits are limited to 48 hours. It is best to plan visits that start on a Friday morning, so students can experience both weekday and weekends on campus. Student-athletes should inform coaches in advance what they hope to see, including classes that are of interest to the student-athlete. Prepare a list of questions for an official visit and check off those questions answered during your tour. Some of the key questions to ask during a visit include:

a.   Academic Questions

What is the typical class size?

What is the typical class schedule?

What is the quality of the campus, dorms, and food services?

What financial aid (non scholarship) is available?

b.   Questions to ask the college or university coach

After your tour of the campus has concluded, ask the coach questions that were not answered during the tour. Below are some sample questions:

How many fall inter squad games are played?

What and when is the practice schedule?

How many exhibition games are played?

What type of conditioning program is available?

What is the quality of the facilities available?

Does the baseball program share fields with other sports?

How many players are on scholarship and at what positions?

How many players will be signed in the coming year?

How many players are at each position and how many will be added the next year?

How many players have transferred or left the program in the past year?

A team with a roster of 35 players allows a new recruit the best chance of playing time. Many programs stockpile players with 40, 50, or up to 60 players, thus limiting the amount of playing time available per player.

c.   **Questions to ask potential teammates**

Try to meet with current players away from the field in order to get a true assessment of the program. Specifically talk with current players who were not on the official tour.

Ask for an honest assessment of the head coach and the assistant coaches. What are they like? What is their temperament?

What is the demand made by staff on a player's schedule?

How good is the conditioning program? Did it meet the player's expectations?

What is the attitude of the other players on the team? Are they cooperative, confrontational, negative, cut throat, supportive, disenchanted?

Why did the player chose to play at that specific college or university?

D.   RECRUITING PROCESS

There are typically four stages in the recruiting process.

First Stage - Recognition. College and university coaches will request information from the student-athlete to build their knowledge base about player. Potential student-athletes should send back as soon as possible any evaluation forms received from a college. Waiting suggests a lack of interest by the student-athlete.

Second Stage - Evaluation. College and university coaches will call the high school coach or travel team coach to learn more about the potential student-athlete. This is a good sign and is evidence that the college or university head coach is interested in the student-athlete.

Third Stage - Recruiting. College and university coaches will contact the potential student-athlete personally to arrange a time to observe the student-athlete play in a high school game or practice. Student-athletes should be ready to answer any questions asked by the coach. Student-athletes also should anticipate that a coach may come unannounced for a drop in visit to evaluate the player's skills.

Fourth Stage - Full Recruiting. The potential student-athlete is invited by the college or university coach for an expense paid official visit to the school.

Early Commitments. A recent development in the college and university baseball recruiting process has been the use of early commitments by coaches for younger high school players-freshmen and sophomores. A college or university coach who utilizes early commitments will offer a scholarship to an eligible player outside the normal recruiting process.

Warning: These early commitments are non-binding and usually involve only a handshake between the potential student-athlete and a head coach. Until a player signs a National Letter of Intent, there is no legal contract between the college or university and the student-athlete. Once a student-athlete indicates a willingness to accept an early commitment offer, other programs will stop recruiting that player. It is wise for a potential student-athlete to obtain legal advice prior to accepting any early commitment offer.

E.   SOBERING STATISTICS

Only 11 percent of high school baseball players go on to play baseball at a college or university. The search for the right school and program takes patience, hard work, and numerous contacts. The following statistics reflect the number of student-athletes who played baseball at a college or university in 2012:

Baseball Programs	Programs	Players
NCAA Division I	297	10,034
NCAA Division II	251	9,220
NCAA Division III	363	11,882
NAIA	194	6,853
NJCAA	388	11,173
Others	150	4,079

Totals:

High School Baseball Players: 474,219

High School Senior Baseball Players: 135,655

Number of College Players: 53,241.

Percentage of High School Players to Professional: .050 percent.[13]

---

[13] Scholarshipstats.com (2012).

CHAPTER 7

SUMMER COLLEGIATE BASEBALL LEAGUES

Collegiate summer wooden bat leagues offer college and university players a chance to continue playing the game during the summer months. There are at least 39 different collegiate summer baseball leagues in the United States and Canada, and a total of 345 teams playing in these leagues. The popularity of college wooden bat leagues continues to grow each year. In 2007, when we published our first summer collegiate league guide, *Wooden Bat Baseball Leagues in America* (Foxhall Road Publications, 2007), we identified 28 such leagues.

Set forth below are the leagues listed by region. The premier leagues in each region are listed first, followed by other leagues in the region. Most of the 39 leagues profiled below meet six different criteria for being considered a major summer collegiate league: the league recruits players nationally as opposed to being local players; each team in the league operates a host family program; the league plays a 35 to 60 game schedule; players are not paid; all players have college eligibility; and the league uses exclusively wooden bats.

A.   NORTHEAST

   1.   **Cape Cod Baseball League**
        capecodbaseball.org

Organized baseball began on Cape Cod as early as 1866. By 1885 each town on Cape Cod had formed town teams which played in tournaments throughout Massachusetts. In 1923, the CCBL was established. The league included ex-minor league players, high school players, and college players. In October 1962, the league appointed its first commissioner and the modern era of Cape Cod baseball

53

began. In 1966 the NCAA certified the CCBL, which allowed college players to play in the league without jeopardizing their amateur status. In 1985 the CCBL became the first summer collegiate league to return to wooden bats for league play.

The CCBL has ten teams, from Orleans in the East to Wareham in the West, a total of 32 miles. The league has two divisions, East and West, and plays a 44 game schedule from June 1 to August 15. All teams in the league are 501(c)(3) non-profit organizations and the league is an approved 501(c)(3) organization (26 U.S.C. § 501). The CCBL is a charter member of the National Alliance of College Summer Baseball and is certified by Major League Baseball.

2.   New England Collegiate Baseball League
necbl.com

The NEBCL was founded in 1993 by George Foster (former Cincinnati Reds and New York Mets All-Star) and Emmy Award winning television producer/director Joseph Consentino. The first commissioner of the league was Fay Vincent (former Commissioner of Major League Baseball). In 2014 the league had 12 teams from Danbury, Connecticut, in the South, to Sanford, Maine, in the North. The league is divided into two Divisions, East and West, and plays a 44 game league season from June 1 to August 10. The league is an approved 501(c)(3) organization and there are a mix of non-profit and for-profit franchises in the league.

3.   New York Collegiate Baseball League
nycbl.com

The NYCBL was founded in 1978 with 14 teams stretching across upper New York. In 2010 seven teams left the NYCBL to form the PGCBL. In 2014 the NYCBL had 13 teams located in Central New York. The league plays a 40 game season from June 1 to July 22. All franchises and the league are approved 501(c)(3) organizations. The NYCBL is a member of the National Alliance of College Summer Baseball and is certified by Major League Baseball.

4. Perfect Game Collegiate Baseball League
pgcbl.com

The PGCBL was founded in 2010 when eight teams from the New York Collegiate League left to form a league with teams located in upstate New York. The league operates in conjunction with Perfect Game USA. In 2014, the league had nine teams located in New York and Northern New Jersey. All the teams in the league are for-profit teams and the league is owned and operated by Perfect Game USA.

5. Futures Collegiate Baseball League
thefuturesleague.com

The FCBL began operation in 2011 with five franchises. The founders of the league were FCBL ownership groups from the Brockton Rox (Can-Am League) and the Lowell Spinners (Single A affiliate Boston Red Sox). In 2012, the league added five expansion franchises. The league plays a 54 game schedule from June 1 to August 1. All the teams in the league are for-profit organizations. In 2014 the league fielded ten teams playing in four New England states.

B. MID-ATLANTIC

1. Cal Ripken Collegiate Baseball League
calripkenleague.org

The CRCBL was founded in 2005 and entered into an agreement with the Cal Ripken, Sr. Foundation to honor Cal Ripken, Sr., and Cal Ripken, Jr. Two charter members, Bethesda Big Train (2012 Perfect Game) and Youse's Orioles (five AAABA titles), have combined to capture six national titles. The league has 10 teams located in Maryland, Northern Virginia, and the District of

Columbia. The league plays a 42 game schedule from June 1 to August 10. The longest travel distance between teams is Herndon, Virginia, to Baltimore, Maryland, a total of 56 miles. The teams and the league are approved 501(c)(3) organizations. The CRCBL is a member of the National Alliance of College Summer Baseball and is certified by Major League Baseball.

2. Valley Baseball League
valleyleaguebaseball.com

Founded in 1961, the VBL consists of 12 teams located in Virginia's Shenandoah Valley. The VBL has two divisions, North and South, and plays a 42 game schedule from June 1 to August 1. The longest travel distance between teams is from Covington to Warrenton, which is 178 miles. The teams and the league are approved 501(c)(3) organizations. The VBL is a charter member of the National Alliance of College Summer Baseball and is certified by Major League Baseball.

3. Atlantic Collegiate Baseball League
acbl-online.com

The ACBL was founded in 1967 and consists of eight teams located in New Jersey, New York, and Pennsylvania. The league plays a 40 game schedule from June 1 to July 28. The longest travel distance between teams is Allentown, Pennsylvania, to Staten Island, New York, a total of 87 miles. The teams and the league are approved 501(c)(3) organizations and the league is a member of the National Alliance of College Summer Baseball. The ABCL is certified by Major League Baseball.

4. Beach Collegiate Baseball League
beachcollegiatebaseball.com

The BCBL is located in Myrtle Beach, South Carolina. In 2014 there were 16 teams in the league.

5.   **Hamptons Collegiate Baseball League**
      hamptonsbaseball.org

Located on Eastern Long Island, there are seven teams in the HCBL. The league plays a 40 game schedule from June 1 to July 30. The HCBL is a member of the National Alliance of College Summer Baseball and is funded in part by Major League Baseball.

C.   SOUTHEAST

1.   **Coastal Plain League** - coastalplain.com

The CPL was founded in 1997 by Pete Brock and consists of 14 teams located in Southern Virginia, North Carolina and South Carolina. The league plays a 42 game schedule from May 29 to August 14 and is divided into two divisions, East and West. The teams and the league are for-profit organizations. The longest road trip between teams is Columbia, South Carolina, to Petersburg, Virginia, a total of 350 miles. As of 2012, the CPL had over 1,000 alumni drafted to play professional baseball and 57 alumni had played for Major League teams.

2.   **Florida Collegiate Baseball League**
      floridaleague.com

The FCBL was founded in 2003 and consists of seven teams located in Central Florida along the I-4 corridor. The league plays a 45 game schedule from late May until early August. In 2012, the FCBL established the Futures Wooden Bat League (FWL) which is a separate league for baseball players who have signed a National Letter of Intent in high school, verbally committed, or currently play college baseball. The FWL offers college level competition on the same fields used by the FCBL. The FWL plays a 25 game season. The teams and the league are approved 501(c)(3) organizations. The FCBL is a member of the National Alliance of College Summer Baseball and is certified by Major League Baseball.

3.   **Southern Collegiate Baseball League** - scbl.org

The SCBL was founded in 1999 and in 2014 consisted of five teams located in Central North Carolina and South Carolina. The longest distance between teams is from Ashville, North Carolina, to Spartanburg, South Carolina, a total of 65 miles. The league plays a 42 game schedule in June and July each year. The SCBL maintains an 85-pitch count for pitchers, plays doubleheaders on weekends, and two games during the week. The teams and league are approved 501(c)(3) organizations. The SCBL is a member of the National Alliance of College Summer Baseball and is certified by Major League Baseball.

4.   **Carolina-Virginia Collegiate League** - cvscl.com

The CVCL is a ten team league located in Virginia and North Carolina. Teams play a 40 game schedule from May 23 to August 1.

5.   **Cotton States Baseball League**
cottonstatesleague.com

The CSBL is a six team league located in Mississippi. The league plays a 28 game schedule in June and July. The league does not have host families and players typically reside within 150 miles of the league teams.

6.   **Sunbelt Collegiate Baseball League**
sunbeltleague.com

The SCBL is a 12 team league located in the Metro Atlanta area. The league operates three divisions.

D.   MIDWEST

   1.   **Northwoods League** - northwoodsleague.com

   The NWL began in 1994 and has grown to 18 teams located in Wisconsin, Minnesota, Iowa, Michigan, and Ontario. The longest distance between teams is Waterloo, Iowa, to Ontario, Canada, a total of 650 miles. Teams are organized into two divisions and play a 70 game schedule from May 27 to August 15. All travel between games is by charter bus. The league is owned by the Northwoods League Foundation, an approved 501(c)(3) organization and the teams are individually owned for-profit organizations. In 2014 the NWL led all collegiate summer baseball leagues in attendance with over one million fans.

   2.   **Great Lakes Summer Collegiate League** greatlakesleague.org

   Founded in 1986, the GLSCL has 12 teams located in Kentucky, Ohio, and Michigan. The longest distance between teams is 322 miles. The league plays a 40 game schedule in June and July. The teams and the league are approved 501(c)(3) organizations. The GLCBL is a member of the National Alliance of College Summer Baseball and is certified by Major League Baseball.

   3.   **Prospect League** - prospectleague.com

   Originally founded in 1963, a new Prospects League was founded in 2008 and consists of 12 teams divided into two divisions located in Missouri, Illinois, Indiana, Ohio, Pennsylvania, New York, and West Virginia. The longest drive between teams is 683 miles, from Hannibal, Missouri, to Butler, Pennsylvania. All teams travel by charter bus and the league plays a 60 game schedule from May 29 to August 14. The teams and league are for-profit organizations.

4.   **M.I.N.K Collegiate Summer Baseball League**
minkleaguebaseball.com

Founded in 1910, the league has eight teams located in Missouri, Iowa, Nebraska, and Kansas. Teams play a 42 game schedule in June and July. The league is a member of the National Baseball Congress.

5.   **Jay Hawk Baseball League**
jayhawkbaseballleague.org

Founded in 1976, the JHBL has eight teams located in Kansas. The league has utilized wooden bats since 1991. The league is a member of the National Baseball Congress.

6.   **Midwest Collegiate League**
midwestcollegiateleague.com

Founded in 2010, the MCL consists of seven teams located in Illinois. The MCL plays a 45 game season beginning on May 30 and ending August 1. The league is a member of the National Amateur Baseball Federation. The teams and the league are for-profit corporations.

7.   **Ohio Valley League** - ohiovalleyleague.net

The OVL was founded in 2011 with three teams from the former KIT League. The OVL consists of five teams in Kentucky and Indiana. In 2013, the Dubois County Bombers moved from the Prospect League to the OVL. Teams play a 45 game schedule in June and July.

8.   **St. Louis Metro Collegiate Instructional Baseball League** - stlcollegebaseball.com

Founded in 1980, the Metro League consists of six teams in the St. Louis area. The league is for players between the ages of 19 and 22. The league is a member of the National Amateur Baseball Federation.

9. **Tri State Collegiate League** - tsclb.com

Founded in 2006 , the TSCL has ten teams located in Northern Ohio and Western Pennsylvania. Many of the TSCL teams were members of the short lived Erie Shores Collegiate League. The league is a member of the National Amateur Baseball Federation.

10. **Lake Michigan Baseball League**

Founded 2013, the league has six teams in the Chicago area that play a 24 game schedule.

11. **Walter Johnson League** - wjbaseball.com

The Walter Johnson League consists of eight teams located in Kansas. The league is a member of the National Baseball Congress.

E. SOUTHWEST

1. **Texas Collegiate League**
texascollegiateleague.com

Founded in 2004, the TCL consists of seven teams located in Western Louisiana and Central Texas. The teams play a 60 game schedule from May 30 to August 1. The league is owned by the Haddock Foundation, a 501(c)(3) organization, and the member clubs are for-profit corporations.

2. **Arizona Collegiate Wooden Bat League**
azsummerball.com/league

The league consists of 15 teams playing from June 1 to August 15.

3.   **Centex Collegiate Baseball League**
centexbaseballleague.com

The CCBL has eight teams located in Central Texas. The teams play a 28 game schedule in June and July. The league is made up of 70 percent college players, 15 percent high school players, and 15 former professionals.

F.   MOUNTAIN WEST - rmblcolorado.com

Mountain Collegiate Baseball League. The league has 12 teams located in Colorado and Wyoming. The teams are organized as for-profit corporations and play a 41 game season, plus exhibition games. The league is a member of the National Baseball Congress.

G.   WEST COAST

1.   **Alaska Baseball League** - alaskabaseballleague.org

The ABL consists of six teams in southern Alaska. Players must have attended one year of college and have one year of NCAA eligibility remaining. Teams play a 40 game schedule. ABL is a member of the National Baseball Congress.

2.   **California Collegiate League**
calsummerball.com

The CCL has 11 teams located in Southern California. The league plays a 36 game season. Teams and league are non-profit 501(c)(3) organizations. The league is a member of the National Baseball Congress and is funded in part by Major League Baseball.

3.   **Southern California Collegiate Baseball League**
sccbaseball.com

The SCCBL is a six team league that plays in Southern California. The league plays a 16 game conference schedule and an additional 30 to 40 nonconference games.

4. Far West League
farwestleaguesummerbaseball.com

Teams were located in Northern California. Eight teams played a 42 game schedule. The league has ceased operations.

5. Pacific West Baseball League
pacificwestbaseball.com

Founded in 2009, the league's eight teams were located in Northern California and Nevada. The league has ceased operations.

6 Golden State Collegiate League
goldenstatecollegiatebaseballleague.com

Founded in 2012, the league has seven teams playing in the San Francisco Bay area and Nevada.

7. Hawaii Collegiate Baseball League
hawaii-cbl.com

The HCBL had six teams, which play in June and July. The league ceased operations before the 2013 season.

8. Western Baseball Association
westernbaseballassociation.com

Founded in 1998, the league's 12 teams play a 50 game schedule. Teams are located in Southern California and consist of college players and former pros. The league is a member of the National Baseball Congress.

H.   CANADA

Western Major Baseball League - wmbl.ca

Founded in 1948, the league has 11 teams in Western Canada. They play a 46 game schedule.

CHAPTER 8

SUMMER BALL

A.   WHY PLAY IN A SUMMER LEAGUE?

There are three primary reasons why a player should play in a summer collegiate league:

1.   Exposure

2.   Experience using a wooden bat

3.   Chance to improve skills

Summer league play is an opportunity for college players to test their skills in an intense short season against some of the best players in the country. Summer baseball teams are not training camps. Few managers of summer teams try to change a player's batting stance or a pitcher's throwing motion during the summer season. One reason is the season is far too short, typically six to eight weeks. Another is that players on a summer league basically are on loan from the players' respective colleges and summer league managers are hesitant to make such changes unless encouraged to do so by a player's college or university coach.

An integral part of summer league play is the use of a wooden bat. Playing with a wooden bat sharpens a batter's skills. Batters should develop quicker hand speed using a wooden bat and the player's reaction times should be faster as well. One reason for this is an aluminum bat has less weight in the barrel than a wooden bat. This also makes it is easier for a batter to hit an inside pitch. The sweet spot on the baseball bat determines the maximum force and velocity the bat can produce. The sweet spot of a metal alloy bat is larger than that of its wooden counterpart. Most players have difficulty learning to hit an inside pitch using a wooden bat until they have used a wooden bat for at least two weeks. If possible, players should take batting practice using a wooden bat two weeks prior to joining a summer team to improve their chances of performing well earlier in a short summer season. Players should not underestimate the difficulty of switching from aluminum bats to wooden bats.

There are various types of wooden bats and selection of the right type for the specific player is important. If a batter tends to hit the ball off the end of the bat, the player should use a white ash bat because white ash is more forgiving if the batter misses the sweet spot. Maple bats are very dense, so the ball will travel farther if it squarely on the sweet spot. Also, the maple bats typically perform better than ash bats for hits coming off the handle or if a batter gets jammed with an inside pitch.

B   HOW TO JOIN A SUMMER COLLEGIATE TEAM

There are a number of ways to join a summer collegiate baseball team. The most effective way is for the player's college coach to recommend the player to a summer team coach. Referrals for summer teams begin in September of the previous year. A player should determine who on the their college team's coaching staff is assigned to place players for the summer leagues and contact that coach in mid-August of the year prior to the specific summer league season. Although the recruitment period for summer leagues runs from September to May, most premier collegiate summer league teams obtain player contracts as early as September or October of the year prior to the summer season. Because there are over 13,000 college baseball players who participate in NCAA Division I, II, and III, NAIA, and junior college programs vying for a limited number of summer team slots, players interested in joining a summer league team must be proactive to insure placement on a team.

Another way to join a summer league team is for players to determine themselves the league or team they are interested in and to

66

contact the league or team directly. The contact information and email addresses of most summer league teams typically is available from the specific team and league websites (See Chapter 7). Personal emails directed to a specific team or coach are more likely to get a response than emails directed to leagues, or a number of leagues, addressed only "To Whom it May Concern." Accordingly, rather than send a general email to all teams in a league, try to reach out to specific teams. And remember, it is not unusual for coaches or teams within a league to share recruiting info throughout the recruiting season, helping other teams fill out their rosters.

Emails should include basic information about the player, as well as links to the player's stats from the college or university and any videos that might be available. Sometimes parents of players send recruitment emails on behalf of their college player.

Few summer teams conduct tryouts. A major reason for this is that most teams shut down operations soon after the summer season is over, so typically there is no mechanism in place for tryouts until a week or so before the start of the next season. If summer teams do hold tryouts prior to the season, that information should be available from the team or league website.

Players who do not get selected in the fall prior to the start of the summer season still have a chance of playing for a team the following summer. It is not unusual for up to 20 percent of a team to be added during the spring, prior to the end of the college season, because of players being dropped from the summer rosters. Reasons for this include injury during the college season, players who must attend summer school to maintain scholarships, ineligibility, and personal, family-related issues. Players still looking for a summer league team in the spring should contact specific team coaches directly via email to increase their chances of being added to the roster.

One example of a late summer league signing that paid off for the player happened in 2006 when Charlie Lenhard, a player from the University of Akron, planned to play in a Midwest League. The summer league experienced financial difficulties and Lenhard found himself was without a summer team. Lenhard contacted the head coach for the Silver Spring-Takoma Thunderbolts in late winter and informed the coach of his status. Lenhard kept in contact with the coach over the next several months and, by late May, an opening on the Thunderbolts roster occurred and Lenhard was invited to join the team. That season, Lenhard was named the Cal Ripken Collegiate Baseball League's Co-MVP. Lenhard's persistence paid off.

C.   HOST FAMILIES

Most summer league teams have some type of program that assists out of town players in finding a place to stay for the summer. For most summer league teams, that assistance comes in the form of host families. A host family typically is a person, couple, or family who have extra space in their home, which they offer to make available to the summer league team.

Host families typically agree to provide for the player a clean, safe, and pleasant place to sleep (preferably a separate room as opposed to a spot on the couch), with access to a bathroom. Some teams ask their host families to provide food, typically one meal per day for the player, which usually is breakfast because that is the one meal where the player may still be in the house. It is important that the host family and the player contact each other as soon as possible after host families are assigned. The player's parents also are encouraged to contact the player's host family to help insure a smooth transition for the player. Players and families should exchange contact and emergency information, as well as a description of the home and the members of the family.

In addition to being courteous and appreciative of host families, players should make sure they spend some quality time with their host families. Remember, most host families invite players into their homes because they love the game of baseball. If a family has children, players should strive to spend time with the children, talk baseball, watch it together on the television, or play it in the back yard. Players should share their experiences with the family. By the end of the summer, the player and the host family truly should feel like family.

CHAPTER 9

COLLEGE BALL AND BEYOND

Once a student-athlete makes a college baseball team, the hard work has just begun. Sometimes the team and player are not the right fit; sometimes the player gets hurt early in his college career; sometimes a player is approached by an agent wanting to represent the player. This section addresses issues that may arise after the student-athlete makes the team. .

A.   REDSHIRT

The term redshirt refers to a suspension or delay that extends the length of a student-athlete's eligibility as an active player.

1.   Period of Eligibility

As a general rule, the following periods of eligibility apply to a student-athlete.

NCAA Division I players must complete four seasons of eligibility within a consecutive five year period (NCAA 5 Year Rule).

NCAA Division II and Division III players must complete four seasons of eligibility within 10 consecutive semesters or 15 quarters.

NAIA players must complete four seasons of eligibility in 10 semesters, or 12 trimesters, or 15 quarters, which do not need to be consecutive (NAIA 10 Semester Rule).

NJCAA players must complete two seasons of eligibility within a two year consecutive time period.

NWAACC and CCCAA players must complete two seasons of eligibility within a two year consecutive time period.

USCA players are limited to four seasons of competition in the same sport. The Association allows a player to request a one year leave of absence.

NCCAA players must complete four seasons of eligibility within 10 semesters, or 12 trimesters or 15 quarters which do not need to be consecutive.

2.   **Extensions of Eligibility Period**

The length of the redshirt period is typically one calendar year, but can be extended. There are a number of redshirt options that allow a player to extend his period of eligibility.

a.   Redshirt Undergraduate Student

Commonly referred to as a "hardship waiver" or "medical redshirt, " a redshirt undergraduate student waiver is available to a student-athlete who, due to an injury or illness, is not able to play the entire season or part of a season. The medical redshirt rules for each association provide that a student-athlete may petition their conference or designated committee for a waiver:

NCAA - Petition conference commissioner or file request with the NCAA Committee on Student Athlete Reinstatements.

NAIA - Apply to NAIA National Office.

NJCAA- Request filed with NJCAA Office of Eligibility.

CCCAA - File request with Conference Commissioner.

NWAACC - File request with national office.

USCAA - File request with USCAA National Office.

b.   One Year Waiver

A one year waiver may be granted to a student-athlete if :

NCAA - the injury or illness was (a) season ending, (b) happened in the first half of the season and, (c) the student-athlete has participated in less than four scheduled competitions during the season or no more than 30 percent of the team's games (whichever is greater).

NAIA - the injury or illness was (a) season ending, (b) happened in the first half of the season and, (c) the student-athlete has participated in no more than eight scheduled games in a season.

NJCAA,CCCAA, NWAACC - the injury or illness occurred (a) in first half of regular season and (b) the student-athlete has not participated in 20 percent of the regular season games or two scheduled games, whichever is greater.

USCAA - injury or illness (a) discontinued the student-athlete's season and (b) the student-athlete has not competed in more than 30 percent of the scheduled games in that season.

Typically, the medical redshirt rules allow student-athletes to complete their academic program beyond five years without sacrificing their eligibility to play. A redshirted student-athlete can practice and play in a scrimmage with his team, but if he plays in one inning of a game during the redshirt period after the waiver has been granted, the waiver will be revoked.[14]

---

[14] Medical redshirt - NCAA, Bylaws 14.2.4, Committee on Student-Athlete Reinstatements; USCAA, Eligibility Guidelines Hardship Form, NAIA, Guide For College Bound Student Athlete (www.playnaia.org), NJCAA, Eligibility Rules, Section 8, Hardship (njcaa.org); CCCAA, Bylaws (2014-15) Bylaw 1.

c.   Redshirt Graduate Student

A redshirted student-athlete in a NCAA Division I program who competes as a graduate student, must remain at the same school. A NCAA Division II graduate student can play at another school.

d.   Academic Redshirt

The new NCAA bylaw changes (effective 2016) require a student-athlete to complete 16 core courses during his high school years and 10 of these core courses must be completed by the start of the senior year in high school. (See Chapter 2, Eligibility). The old standard allowed student-athletes to complete all of the core courses by the end of their senior year and maintain a minimum GPA of 2.0 based on a sliding scale. Those student athletes who fall between the old eligibility standard and the new standard (post 2016) may be eligible for an academic redshirt. The student-athlete will be allowed to practice with a team his first year while he completes the core courses and play the following season as an academic redshirt.

The student-athlete must complete nine credit hours of college courses in the first semester to be eligible.[15]

e.   Roster Designations

Many college and university baseball teams list their redshirt players on the roster. The following designations are used: "RSR" - redshirt senior; "RJR" - redshirt junior; "RSO" - redshirt sophomore/freshman.

A redshirt may be granted to a student athlete at any time during their college or university eligibility period. A redshirt player is eligible to receive his scholarship during the redshirt period.

---

[15] Academic Redshirt - Mita, Sherman, New Eligibility Standards on the Way (espn.go.com), May 3, 2012.

B.   TRANSFERS

A student-athlete currently attending an NCAA Division I or Division II school needs written permission from the program's athletic director to contact another college or university head coach or staff to discuss a possible transfer. Without this permission, the head coach may not talk with the student-athlete or his parents about a possible transfer to that program. For NCAA Division III programs, the student-athlete can issue his own release (called a self release). The form for a self release is available on the NCAA website. Once the form is submitted pursuant to the procedures set forth on the NCAA website, the student-athlete may contact the head coach of another college or university program.

There are three types of transfers:

1.   **Two Year College To Four Year College or University (2-4 Transfer)**

a.   NCAA Division I

A student-athlete considering a transfer to a NCAA Division I program should first register with the NCAA Eligibility Center to determine if the student-athlete is a qualified, partial qualified, or non-qualified status student. A qualified student-athlete can transfer anytime and play the following season. A non-qualified student-athlete cannot transfer after his first year and will need to complete course work before he is eligible to transfer. If a player completes a fall season of baseball he is ineligible to play the following season.

b.   NCAA Division II

A student-athlete can transfer to a NCAA Division II program after freshman year if the student-athlete has completed two full semesters and has a minimum GPA of 2.0. The student-athlete is eligible to play the following spring.

c.   NAIA Transfer

There are no restrictions on transfers from a two year college to an NAIA college.

2.   **Transfers From A Four Year College or University To Another Four Year College or University (4-4 Transfer)**

For NCAA Division I and NAIA, the basic transfer rule is that a student-athlete must "sit out" for an entire school year and must be enrolled in two full semesters at a school before a student-athlete can play at the transfer school. There are a number of exceptions to this rule.

a.   Sport Discontinued

If a college or university discontinues support of a baseball program, the student-athlete can transfer to an NCAA or NAIA college or university and play the following season.

b.   Student-Athlete Never Was Recruited

If a student-athlete was not recruited by the NCAA Division I, Division II, or NAIA school where the player wishes to transfer, then the basic rule does not apply, as long as the student-athlete, although a member of the team, did not receive an athletic scholarship and did not participated in intercollegiate games prior to the transfer .

c.   Potential Student-Athlete Never Played Sport

If a player never played or practiced with a team (high school or college) for two years prior to the transfer, the player is exempt from the basic transfer rule.

d.   Transfer To A Division III School

If a student-athlete seeks to transfer to a NCAA Division III school from a NCAA Division I, NCAA Division II, or NAIA college or university, the student-athlete is exempt from the basic transfer rule if the student-athlete is academically eligible at his current college or university.

e.   One-Time Transfer Rule

If a NCAA Division I student-athlete wishes to transfer to a NCAA Division II college or university, the student-athlete will be exempt from the basic transfer rule if the player-athlete is academically eligible at the his current college or university and obtains a written statement from his current college or university allowing for a one time release. This exception only applies to transfers from a NCAA Division I program to a NCAA Division II program.

f.   NAIA Exceptions

If an NAIA student-athlete wishes to transfer to another NAIA college or university, the student-athlete can compete immediately if the student-athlete obtains a written release from the college or university from which he transferred, or if the student-athlete registered at the transfer college or university at least 16 consecutive weeks prior to playing baseball at the transfer college or university.[16]

3.   **CCCA and NWAACC Transfers**

NWAAC requires a student-athlete to complete and pass 12 quarter credit hours of classes and have a cumulative 2.0 GPA from a two year or four year program outside Oregon or Washington in order to play immediately at a NWAAC transfer college.

---

[16] Transfers - Transfer 101, NCAA 2014-15.

Any student-athlete transferring from a two year or four year college outside of California to a CCCA college must complete 24 semester units and have a cumulative 2.0 GPA.

C.   WALK-ONS

Most NCAA Division I, Division II, Division III, NAIA, and NJCAA programs offer some form of walk-on tryouts or player previews in the early fall. The number of walk-on candidates who make the team is dictated by the number of scholarship and roster positions on an individual team. NCAA Division I programs are limited to 35 roster spots. For Division I, Division II, Division III, NAIA, and NJCAA programs, the roster size is limited by the individual conferences (e.g., the Sunbelt Conference limits baseball rosters to 41 players for conference playoffs). A NCAA Division I program can spread out its allotment of scholarships for up to 27 players.[17] Thus, at Division I programs, there potentially are eight roster spots open which can be filled from walk-on players.

There are two types of college or university baseball walk-ons:

1.   **Recruited Walk-On**

A recruited walk-on is a player who has been asked to try out for the team, but has not been recruited by a coach for a scholarship. A recruited walk-on will receive team information over the summer and be directly informed by a coach of the workout dates in early September.

2.   **Direct Walk-On**

A direct walk-on is a player who was not contacted by a coach, or player who changes schools after his first year (and otherwise meets the eligibility requirements for transfers). This player

---

[17] NCAA Baseball Rules (2014).

will need to be persistent in obtaining information regarding the date of the tryout.

Several Major League players were former walk-on players while at their respective college or university. Eric Karros walked-on to UCLA's baseball team and later played with the Los Angeles Dodgers. Bret Gardiner walked-on to the College of Charleston and went on to be drafted and play with the New York Yankees. Ozzie Smith walked-on to the Cal Poly-San Luis Obispo team and became a Hall of Fame player with the St. Louis Cardinals.

3.   **Tips For A Successful Walk-On Tryout**

a.   Contact the head coach in the summer prior to freshman year and express interest in trying out for the team. Ask when the tryout will be, including date, time, and place.

b.   Prior to the tryout, refine one or two key skill areas to "show off" at the tryout (e.g., superior defensive skills, great base running skills, or a great curve ball). The time frame to impress the coach is short (maybe less than 5 minutes).

c.   Before the tryout, get plenty of rest.

d.   Contact players currently on the team and ask questions about the team, such as which player position need to be filled, are there any holes in the current lineup, is the coach an offense or defense oriented coach.

e.   Make a short video (less than 3 minutes) of key skill areas to give to the coach at the tryout (See Chapter 4, Section B). Coaches often times will review such video as soon as the tryouts are over.

D.   MAJOR LEAGUE BASEBALL DRAFT

The First Year Player Draft (also known as the Amateur Draft or the Rule 4 Draft) is held each year in early June. There are

40 rounds each year. Players selected in the draft must be signed by the club on or before the Friday between July 11-18 at 5 p.m. If a player does not sign with the club by that time, the player is ineligible to play affiliated professional baseball that season.

1.   **Eligible Draft Players**

To be eligible for the draft:, a player must:

a.   Be a resident of the United States, Canada, or a U.S. territory such as Puerto Rico. Players from other countries are not subject to the draft, and can be signed by any team unless they are current members of a college team.

b.   Never have signed a professional contract (either major or minor league contract).

High school players are eligible to be drafted only the summer after their high school graduation, and only if they have not attended college. Players attending four-year colleges or universities are eligible after completing their junior year, or after their 21st birthday. Junior college and community college players are eligible to be drafted at any time regardless of the number of college years completed.[18]

2.   **Negotiation List**

A player who has been selected by a team during the draft is placed on that team's negotiation list. As noted above. the major league club has until the Friday between July 12-18 at 5:00 p.m. to sign that player to a contract (the contract can only be a minor league contract). If a club does not sign the player, he becomes eligible for selection in the next year's draft, unless he is a graduating college senior. A drafted player will remain on the club's negotiation list until

---

[18] angelfire.com/prospectwatch/draft.

one week before the next draft, or until the player signs with that club.[19]

3.   Non-Drafted Player

If a player is not selected during the draft, he becomes a Non-Drafted Free-Agent (NDFA) or an Undrafted Free Agent. For NDFA high school players, the player can be signed by any club after the draft, but before the player enrolls in a college. Thus, a high school player has two options: see if he is drafted in early June (he has until mid-July to sign a contract) or wait until late August before registering with a college to see if he can sign a contract with a team as a NDFA player. Clubs are not allowed to select a player two years in a row, unless they receive written approval from the player prior to the draft.[20]

---

[19] www.thecubreporter.com/book/expert/expert/htm/3551.
[20] Ibid.

LIST OF APPENDICES

Appendix 1 - Colleges And Universities By Organization And Division

APPENDIX 1

Colleges And Universities By Organization And Division

I.   NCAA Division I Baseball Colleges/Universities

CONFERENCE/ SCHOOL	WEBSITE	STATE

A.   American East Conf. - americaeast.com

Albany University	ualbanysports.com	NY
Binghamton University	bubearcats.com	NY
University of Hartford	hartfordhawks.com	CT
University of Maine	goblackbears.com	ME
University of Maryland - Baltimore County	umbcretrievers.com	MD
University of Mass. - Lowell	goriverhawks.com	MA
Stony Brook University	goseawolves.org	NY

B.   The American Conf. - theamerican.org

University of Cincinnati	gobearcats.com	OH
University of Connecticut	uconnhuskies.com	CT
University of Central Florida	ucfknights.com	FL
Georgetown University	guhoyas.com	DC
University of Houston	uhcougars.com	TX
University of Louisville	gocards.com	KY
University of Memphis	gotigersgo.com	TN
St. John's University	redstormsports.com	NY
Seton Hall University	shupirates.com	NJ
Temple University	owlsports.com	PA
University of South Florida	gousfbulls.com	FL

Villanova University   villanova.com   PA

C. **Atlantic Coast Conf.** - theacc.com

Boston College	bceagles.com	MA
Clemson University	clemsontigers.com	SC
Duke University	goduke.com	NC
Florida State University	seminoles.com	FL
Georgia Tech	ramblinwreck.com	GA
University of Miami	hurricanesports.com	FL
University of North Carolina	goheels.com	NC
North Carolina State University	gopack.com	NC
University of Notre Dame	und.com	IN
University of Pittsburgh	pittsburghpanthers.com	PA
Syracuse University	suathletics.syr.edu	NY
University of Virginia	virginiasports.com	VA
Virginia Tech Hokies	hokiesports.com	VA
Wake Forest University	wakeforestsports.com	NC

D. **Atlantic Sun Conf.** - atlanticsun.org

East Tennessee State University	etsubucs.com	TN
Florida Gulf Coast University	fgcuathletics.com	FL
Jacksonville University	judolphins.com	FL
Kennesaw State University	ksuowls.com	GA
Lipscomb University	lipscombsports.com	TN
Mercer University	mercerbears.com	GA
Northern Kentucky University	nkunorse.com	KY
University of North Florida	unfospreys.com	FL
University of South Carolina - Upstate	upstatespartans.com	SC
Stetson University	gohatters.com	FL

E.   **Atlantic 10 Conf.** - atlantic10.com

University of Dayton	daytonflyers.com	OH
Davidson University	davidsonwildcats.com	NC
Fordham University	fordhamsports.com	NY
George Washington University	gwsports.com	DC
La Salle University	goexplorers.com	PA
University of Massachusetts	umassathletics.com	MA
University of Rhode Island	gorhody.com	RI
University of Richmond	richmondspiders.com	VA
St. Bonaventure University	gobonnies.sbu.edu/sports	PA
Saint Joseph's University	sjuhawks.com	PA
Saint Louis University	slubillikens.com	MO
Virginia Commonwealth University	vcuathletics.com	VA

F.   **Big East Conf.** - bigeast.org

Butler University	butlersports.com	IN
Creighton University	gocreighton.com	NE
Georgetown University	guhoyas.com	DC
St. John's University	redstormsports.com	NY
Seaton Hall University	shupirates.com	NY
Villanova University	villanova.com	PA

G.   **Big South Conf.** - bigsouthsports.com

Campbell University	gocamels.com	SC
Charleston Southern University	csusports.com	SC
Coastal Carolina University	goccusports.com	NC
Gardner-Webb University	gwusports.com	NC
High Point University	highpointpanthers.com	NC
Liberty University	liberty.edu/flames	VA
Longwood University	longwoodlancers.com	NC
Presbyterian College	gobluehose.com	NC

Radford University	ruhighlanders.com	VA
University of North Carolina - Asheville	uncabulldogs.com	NC
Virginia Military Institute	vmikeydets.com	VA
Winthrop University	winthropeagles.com	SC

H.   **Big 10 Conf.** - bigten.org

University of Illinois	fightingillini.com	IL
Indiana University	iuhoosiers.com	IN
University of Iowa	hawkeyesports.com	IO
University of Maryland	umterps.com	MD
University of Michigan	mgoblue.com	MI
Michigan State University	msuspartans.com	MI
University of Minnesota	gophersports.com	MN
University of Nebraska	huskers.com	NE
Northwestern University	nusports.com	IL
Ohio State University	ohiostatebuckeyes.com	OH
Pennsylvania State University	gopsusports.com	PA
Purdue University	purduesports.com	IN
Rutgers, State University Of New Jersey	rutgers.edu	NJ

I.   **Big 12 Conf.** - big12sports.com

Baylor University	baylorbears.com	TX
University of Kansas	kuathletics.com	KS
Kansas State University	kstatesports.com	KS
University of Oklahoma	soonersports.com	OK
Oklahoma State University	okstate.com	OK
University of Texas	texassports.com	TX
Texas Christian University	gofrogs.cstv.com	TX
Texas Tech University	texastech.com	TX
West Virginia University	wvusports.com	WV

J.   **Big West Conf.** - bigwest.org

California Polytechnic State University	gopoly.com	CA
California State University - Fullerton	fullertontitans.com	CA
California State University - Northridge	gomatadors.com	CA
University of Hawaii	hawaiiathletics.com	HA
California State University - Long Beach	longbeachstate.com/sports	CA
University of California - Davis	ucdavisaggies.com	CA
University of California - Irvine	ucirvinesports.com	CA
University of California - Riverside	gohighlanders.com	CA
University of California - Santa Barbara	ucsbgauchos.com	CA

K.   **Colonial Ath. Association** - caasports.com

College of Charleston	cofcsports.com	SC
University of Delaware	bluehens.com	DE
Drexel University	drexeldragons.com	PA
Elon University	elonphoenix.com	NC
Northeastern University	gonu.com	MA
Hofstra University	gohofstra.com	NY
James Madison University	jmusports.com	VA
Towson University	towsontigers.com	MD
University of North Carolina - Wilmington	uncwsports.com	NC
College of William and Mary	tribeathletics.com	VA

L.   **Conf. USA -** conferenceusa.com

East Carolina University	ecupirates.com	NC
Florida International University	fiusports.com	FL
Florida Atlantic University	fausports.com	FL
Marshall University	herdzone.com	WV
Middle Tennessee State University	goblueraiders.com	TN
University of North Carolina - Charlotte	uncc.edu	NC
Louisiana Tech University	latechsports.com	LA
Tulane University	tulanegreenwave.com	LA
Rice University	riceowls.com	TX
University of Southern Mississippi	southernmiss.com	MS
University of Alabama - Birmingham	uabsports.com	AL
University of Texas San Antonio	goutsa.com	TX

M.   **Horizon League -** horizonleague.org

University of Illinois at Chicago	uicflames.com	IL
Valparaiso University	valpoathletics.com	IN
University of Wisconsin - Milwaukee	uwmpanthers.com	WI
Wright State University	wsuraiders.com	OH
Youngstown State University	ysusports.com	OH

N.   **Ivy League -** ivyleaguesports.com

Brown University	brownbears.com	RI
Columbia University	gocolumbialions.com	NY
Cornell University	cornellbigred.com	NY
Dartmouth College	dartmouthsports.com	NH
Harvard University	gocrimson.com	MA

University of Pennsylvania	pennathletics.com	PA
Princeton University	goprincetontigers.com	NJ
Yale University	yalebulldogs.com	CT

O. **Metro Atlantic Ath. Conf.** - maacsports.com

Canisius College	canisius.edu/athletics	NY
Fairfield University	fairfieldstags.com	CT
Iona College	Icgaels.com	NY
Manhattan College	gojaspers.com	NY
Marist College	goredfoxes.com	NY
Monmouth University	gomuhawks.com	NJ
Niagara University	purpleeagles.com	NY
Quinnipiac College	quinnipiacbobcats.com	CT
Rider University	gobroncs.com	NJ
Saint Peter's College	saintpeterspeacocks.com	NJ
Siena College	sienasaints.com	NY

P. **Mid American Conf.** - mac-sports.com

University of Akron	gozips.com	OH
Ball State University	bgsufalcons.com	OH
Bowling Green State University	ballstatesports.com	OH
University at Buffalo	buffalobulls.com	NY
Central Michigan University	cmuchippewas.com	MI
Eastern Michigan University	emueagles.com	MI
Kent State University	kentstatesports.com	OH
Miami University	muredhawks.com	OH
Northern Illinois University	niuhuskies.com	IL
Ohio University	ohiobobcats.com	OH
University of Toledo	utrockets.com	OH
Western Michigan University	wmubroncos.com	MI

Q.   **Mid Eastern Athletic Conf.** - meacsports.com

Bethune-Cookman University	bcuathletics.com	FL
Coppin State University	coppinstatesports.com	MD
Delaware State University	dsuhornets.com	DE
Florida A&M University	famuathletics.com	FL
University of Maryland - Eastern Shore	umeshawks.com	MD
Norfolk State University	nsuspartans.com	VA
North Carolina A&T University	ncataggies.com	NC
North Carolina Central University	nccueaglepride.com	NC
Savannah State University	ssuathletics.com	GA

R.   **Missouri Valley Conf.** - mvc-sports.com

Bradley University	bradleybraves.com	IL
Dallas Baptist University	dbupatriots.com	TX
Creighton University	Gocreighton.com	NE
University of Evansville	gopurpleaces.com	IN
Illinois State University	goredbirds.com	IL
Indiana State University	gosycamores.com	IN
Missouri State University	missouristatebears.com	MO
Southern Illinois University	siusalukis.com	IL
Wichita State University	goshockers.com	KS

S.   **Mountain West Conf.** - themwc.com

Air Force Academy	goairforcefalcons.com	CO
Fresno State University	gobulldogs.com	CA
University of Nevada-Las Vegas	unlvrebels.com	NV
University of Nevada	nevadawolfpack.com	NV
University of New Mexico	golobos.com	NM
San Diego State University	goaztecs.cstv.com	CA

T.   **Northeast Conf.** - northeastconference.org

Bryant University	bryantbulldogs.com	MA
Central Conn. State University	ccsubluedevils.com	CT
Fairleigh Dickinson University	fduknights.com	PA
Long Island University	liuathletics.com	NY
Monmouth University	gomuhawks.com	NJ
Mount St. Mary's University	mountathletics.com	MD
Sacred Heart University	sacredheartpioneers.com	CT
Wagner College	wagnerathletics.com	NY

U.   **Ohio Valley Conf.** - ovcsports.com

Austin Peay State University	apsugovernors.com	TN
Belmont University	belmontbruins.com	TN
Eastern Illinois University	eiupanthers.com	IL
Eastern Kentucky University	ekusports.com	KY
Jacksonville State University	jsugamecocksports.com	FL
Morehead State University	msueagles.com	MO
Murray State University	goracers.com	KY
Southeast Missouri State University	gosoutheast.com	MO
Southern Illinois University - Edwardsville	siuecougars.com	IL
University of Tennessee Martin	utmsports.com	TN
Tennessee Technological University	ttusports.com	TN

V.   **Pacific 12 Conf.** - pac-12.com

University of Arizona	arizonawildcats.com	AR
Arizona State University	thesundevils.com	AR
University of California	calbears.com	CA
University of Oregon	goducks.com	OR
Oregon State University	osubeavers.com	OR

Stanford University	gostanford.com	CA
University of Cal. Los Angeles	uclabruins.com/sports	CA
University of Colorado	cubuffs.com	CO
University Southern California	usctrojans.com	CA
University of Utah	utahutes.cstv.com/sports	UT
University of Washington	gohuskies.com/sports	WA
Washington State University	wsucougars.com/sports	WA

W. **Patriot League** - patriotleague.org

United States Military Academy	goarmysports.com	NY
Bucknell University	bucknellbison.com	PA
College of the Holy Cross	goholycross.com	MA
Lafayette College	goleopards.com	PA
Lehigh University	lehighsports.com	PA
United States Naval Academy	navysports.com	MD

X. **Southeastern Conf.** - secdigitalnetwork.com

University of Alabama	rolltide.com	AL
University of Arkansas	arkansasrazorbacks.com	AR
Auburn University	auburntigers.com	AL
University of Florida	gatorzone.com	FL
University of Georgia	georgiadogs.com	GA
University of Kentucky	ukathletics.com	KY
Louisiana State University	lsusports.net	LA
University of Mississippi	olemisssports.com	MS
Mississippi State University	hailstate.com	MS
University of Missouri	mutigers.com	MO
University of South Carolina	gamecocksonline.com	SC
University of Tennessee	utsports.com	TN
Texas A&M University	aggieathletics.com	TX
Vanderbilt University	vucommodores.com	TN

Y. **Southern Conf.** - soconsports.com

The Citadel	citadelsports.com	SC
Furman University	furmanpaladins.com	SC
University of North Carolina - Greensboro	uncgspartans.com	NC
Samford University	samfordsports.com	AL
Western Carolina University	catamountsports.com	NC
Wofford College	athletics.wofford.edu	SC
East Tennessee State	etsubucs.com	TN
VMI	vmikeydets.com	VA
Mercer University	mercerbears.com	GA

Z. **Southland Conf.** - southland.org

Abilene Christian University	acusports.com	TX
University of Central Arkansas	ucasports.com	AR
Houston Baptist University	hbuhuskies.com	TX
University of Incarnate Word	uiwcardinals.com	TX
Lamar University	lamarcardinals.com	TX
McNeese State University	mcneesesports.com	LA
Nicholls State University	geauxcolonels.com	LA
University of New Orleans	unoprivateers.com	LA
Northwestern State University	nsudemons.com	LA
Oral Roberts University	orugoldeneagles.com	OK
Sam Houston State University	gobearkats.com	TX
Southeastern Louisiana University	lionsports.net	LA
Stephen F. Austin State University	sfajacks.cstv.com	TX
Texas A&M University - Corpus Christi	goislanders.com	TX

AA. Southwestern Athletic Conf. - swac.org

Alabama A&M University	aamusports.com	AL
Alabama State University	bamastatesports.com	AL
Alcorn State University	alcornsports.com	MS
University of Arkansas at Pine Bluff	uapblionsroar.com	AR
Grambling State University	gsutigers.com	LA
Jackson State University	jsutigers.com	MS
Mississippi Valley State University	mvsusports.com	MS
Prairie View A&M University	pvpanthers.com	TX
Southern University	gojagsports.com	LA
Texas Southern University	athletics.tsu.edu	TX

BB. The Summit League - thesummitleague.org

Indiana University Fort Wayne	gomastodons.com	IN
North Dakota State University	gobison.com	ND
University of Nebraska Omaha	omavs.com	NE
South Dakota State University	usd.edu	SD
Western Illinois University	goleathernecks.com	IL

CC. Sunbelt Conf. - sunbeltsports.org

Appalachian State University	goasu.com	NC
Arkansas State University	astateredwolves.com	AR
Georgia State University	georgiastatesports.com	GA
Georgia Southern University	wkusports.com	GA
University of Louisiana	ragincajuns.com	LA
University of Louisiana Monroe	ulmwarhawks.com	LA
New Mexico State University	nmstatesports.com	NM
University of South Alabama	usajaguars.com	AL
Troy University	troytrojans.com	AL
University of Texas Arlington	utamavs.com	TX
Western Kentucky University	wkusports.com	KY

Texas State University	txstatebobcats.com	TX
University of Idaho	govandals.com	ID

DD. **West Coast Conf.** - wccsports.com

Brigham Young University	byucougars.com	UT
Gonzaga University	gozags.com	WA
Loyola Marymount University	lmulions.com	CA
Pepperdine University	pepperdinesports.com	CA
University of Portland	portlandpilots.com	OR
University of the Pacific	pacifictigers.com	CA
Saint Mary's College of California	smcgaels.com	CA
University of San Diego	usdtoreros.cstv.com	CA
University of San Francisco	usfdons.com	CA
Santa Clara University	santaclarabroncos.com	CA

EE. **Western Ath. Conf.** - wacsports.com

California State U. Bakersfield	gorunners.com	CA
Chicago State University	gocsucougars.com	IL
Sacramento State University	hornetsports.com	CA
Seattle University	goseattleu.com	WA
University of North Dakota	undsports.com	ND
University of Northern Colorado	uncbears.com	CO
University of Texas-Pan American	utpabroncs.com	TX
Utah Valley University	wolveringreen.com	UT

II. NCAA Division II Baseball Colleges/Universities

A. California Collegiate Ath. Assoc. - goccaa.org

Cal State- Chico University	chicowildcats.com	CA
Cal State Dominquez Hills University	gotoros.com	CA
Cal State East Bay University	eastbaypioneers.com	CA
Cal State LA University	csulaathletics.com	CA
Cal State Monterey University	otterathletics.com	CA
Cal State Poly University	broncoathletics.com	CA
Cal State San Bernardino University	csusbathletics.com	CA
Cal State Stanislaus University	warriorathletics.com	CA
SF State University	sfstategators.com	CA
Sonoma State University	sonomaseawolves.com	CA
UC San Diego University	ucsdtritons.com	CA

B. Central Atlantic Collegiate Conf. - caccathletics.org

Bloomfield College	bcdeacons.com	NJ
Caldwell College	caldwellathletics.com	NJ
Chestnut Hill College	griffinathletics.com	PA
Concordia College	concordiaclippers.com	NY
Dominican College	chargerathletics.com	NY
Felician College	felicianathletics.com	NJ
Nyack College	athletics.nyack.edu	NY
Philadelphia University	philaurams.com	PA
Post University	posteagles.com	CT
University of the Sciences in PA	devilsathletics.com	PA
Wilmington University	wilmu.edu/athletics	DE

C.   **Central Intercollegiate Ath. Assoc.** - theciaa.com

Elizabeth City State University	ecsuvikings.com	NC
Lincoln University	lulions.com	PA
Shaw University	shawbears.com	NC
St. Augustine's University	saintaugfalcons.com	NC
Virginia State University	govsutrojans.com	VA
Winston Salem State University	wssurams.com	NC

D.   **Conf. Carolinas** - conference.carolinas.com

Barton College	bartonbulldogs.com	NC
Belmont Abbey College	abbeyathletics.com	NC
Erskine College	erskinesports.com	SC
Limestone College	golimestonesaints.com	SC
Mount Olive College	moctrojans.com	NC
Pfeiffer College	gofalconsports.com	NC
King College	kingtornado.com	TN
North Greenfield University	ngcrusaders.com	SC

E.   **East Coast Conf.** - eccsports.org

Bridgeport University	ubknights.com	CT
Dowling College	dowlingathletics.com	NY
Molloy College	molloy.edu/athletics.com	NY
St. Thomas Aquinas College	staathletics.com	NY

F.   **Great Lakes Intercollegiate Ath. Conf.** - gliac.org

Ashland University	goashlandeagles.com	OH
University of Findlay	findlay.edu	OH
Grand Valley State University	gvsulakers.com	MI
Hillsdale College	hillsdalechargers.com	MI
Northwood University	gonorthwood.com	MI
Malone University	malonepioneers.com	OH

Ohio Dominican University	ohiodominicanpanthers.com	OH
Saginaw Valley State University	svsucardinals.com	MI
Tiffin University	gotiffindragons.com	OH
Walsh University	walsh.edu/walshathletics	OH
Wayne State University	wsuathletics.com	MI

G. **Great Lakes Valley Conf. -** glvcsports.com

Bellarmine University	athletics.bellarmine.edu	KY
University of Indianapolis	athletics.uindy.edu	IN
Kentucky Wesleyan College	kwcpanthers.com	KY
Lewis University	lewisflyers.com	IL
St. Joseph's College	athletics.saintjoe.edu	IN
University of Wisconsin - Parkside	parksiderangers.com	WI
Drury University	drurypanthers.com	MO
Mckendree University	mckbearcats.com	IL
Maryville University	maryvillesaints.com	MO
Missouri University S&T	minerathletics.com	MO
Quincy University	hawks.quincy.edu	IL
Rockhurst University	rockhursthawks.com	MO
University of Southern Indiana	gousieagles.com	IN
University of Missouri-St. Louis	umsltritons.com	MO
William Jewel College	jewellcardinals.com	MO

H. **Great Northwest Ath. Conf. -** gnacsports.com

Central Washington University	wildcatsports.com	WA
Montana State – Billings University	msubsports.com	MT
Northwest Nazarene University	nnusports.com	ID
Simon Frazier University	athletics.sfu.ca	BC (CA)
St. Martin's University	stmartin.edu	WA

Western Oregon University wouwolves.com OR

I. **Great American Conf.** - greatamericanconference.com

University of Arkansas - Monticello	uamsports.com	AK
Arkansas Tech University	athletics.atu.edu	AK
Northwestern Oklahoma State University	riderangersride.com	OK
Southwestern Oklahoma State University	swosuathletics.com	OK
Harding University	hardingsports.com	AR
Ouachita Baptist University	obutigers.com	AR
Southern Arkansas University	muleriderathletics.com	AR
Southeastern Oklahoma State	gosoutheastern.com	OK
Southern Nazarene University	snuathletics.com	OK
East Central University	ecutigers.com	OK

J. **Gulf South Conf.** - gscsports.org

University of Alabama - Huntsville	uahchargers.com	AL
University of North Alabama	roarlions.com	AL
Valdosta State University	vstateblazers.com	GA
University of West Alabama	uwathletics.com	AL
Union University	uuathletics.com	TN
Christian Brothers University	gobucs.com	TN
University of West Florida	goargos.com	FL
University of West Georgia	uwgsports.com	GA
Delta State University	gostatesman.com	MS
Shorter University	goshorterhawks.com	TN
Lee University (2015)	goleeflames.com	TN

K.   **Heartland Conf.** - heartlandsports.org

University of Arkansas - Ft. Smith	uafortsmithlions.com	AK
Newman University	newmanjets.com	KS
Oklahoma Panhandle State University	opsuaggies.com	OK
Oklahoma Christian University	oceagles.com	OK
St. Edwards University	athletics.stedwards.edu	TX
St. Mary's University	rattlerathletics.com	TX
Texas A&M International University	Godustdevils.com	TX
McMurry University	mcmurrysports.com	TX
University of Texas – Permian Basin	utpbfalcons.com	TX

L.   **Lone Star Conf.** - lonestarconference.org

Abilene Christian University	acusports.com	TX
Angelo State University	angelosports.com	TX
Cameron University	cameronaggies.com	OK
Eastern New Mexico University	goeasternathletics.com	NM
University of Incarnate Word	uiwcardinals.com	TX
Midwestern State University	msumustangs.com	TX
Tarleton State University	tarletonsports.com	TX
Texas A&M-Kingsville University	javelinaathletics.com	TX
West Texas A&M University	gobuffsgo.com	TX

M.   **Mid-America Intercollegiate Ath. Assoc**. - themiaa.com

Emporia State	esuhornets.com	KS
Fort Hays State University	fhsuathletics.com	KS

Missouri Southern State University	mssulions.com	MO
Missouri Western State University	gogriffons.com	MO
Northwest Missouri State University	nwmissouri.edu/sports	MO
Pittsburgh State University	pittstategorillas.com	KS
Southwest Baptist University	sbubearcats.com	MO
Truman State University	trumanbulldogs.com	MO
University of Central Missouri	ucmathletics.com	MO
University of Nebraska-Kearney	lopers.com	NE
Washburn University of Topeka	wusports.com	NE
University of Central Oklahoma	bronchosports.com	OK
Lincoln University	lubluetigers.com	MO
Lindenwood University	lindenwoodlions.com	MO
Northeastern State University	goriverhawksgo.com	OK

N. **Northeast-10 Conf.** - northeast10.org

American International College	aicyellowjackets.com	MA
Assumption College	assumptiongreyhounds.com	MA
Bentley University	bentleyfalcons.com	MA
Franklin Pierce University	athletics.franklinpierce.edu	NH
LeMoyne College	lemoynedolphins.com	NY
Merrimack College	merrimackathletics.com	MA
University of New Haven	newhavenchargers.com	CT
Pace University	pacesuathletics.com	NY
Southern Connecticut State University	southernctowls.com	CT
Southern New Hampshire University	snhupenmen.com	NH
St. Anselm College	saintanselmhawks.com	NH
The College of St. Rose	gogoldenknights.com	NY
Stonehill College	stonehillskyhawks.com	MA
UMass-Lowell	goriverhawks.com	MA

| Adelphi University | aupanthers.com | NY |
| St. Michaels College | smcathletics.com | VT |

O. **Northern Sun Intercollegiate Conf.** - northernsun.org

Augustana College	goaugie.com	SD
Bemidji State University	bsubeavers.com	MN
Concordia University- St. Paul	cugoldenbears.com	MN
Minnesota State University - Mankato	msumavericks.com	MN
Minnesota State University - Moorhead	msumdragons.com	MN
Minot State University	msubeavers.com	ND
Northern State University	northern.edu/athletics.com	SD
Southwest Minnesota State University	smsumustangs.com	MN
St. Cloud State University	scsuhuskies.com	MN
University of Sioux Falls	usfcougars.com	SD
University of Mary	gomary.com	ND
University of Minnesota - Crookston	goldeneaglessports.com	MN
University of Minnesota Duluth	umdbulldogs.com	MN
Upper Iowa University	uperiowaathletics.com	IA
Wayne State College	wscwildcats.com	NE
Winona State University	winonastatewarriors.com	MN

P. **Pacific West Conf.**   pacificwestsports.org

Academy of Art University	artuathletics.com	CA
Azusa Pacific	apu.edu/athletics	CA
Dixie State University	dixieathletics.com	UT
Grand Canyon University	gculopes.com	AZ
University of Hawaii – Hilo	hiloathletics.com	HI
California Baptist University	cbulancers.com	CA

Fresno Pacific University	fpuathletics.com	CA
Point Loma Nazarene University	plnusealions.com	CA
Hawaii Pacific University	hpusharks.com	HI
Holy Names University	hnuhawks.com	CA

Q. **Peach Belt Conf.** - peachbelt.com

Armstrong Atlantic University	armstrongpirates.com	GA
Augusta State University	jaguarsroar.com	GA
Columbus State University	csucougars.com	GA
Flagler College	flaglerathletics.com	FL
Francis Marion University	fmupatriots.com	SC
Georgia College & State University	gcsubobcats.com	GA
Georgia Southwestern University	gswcanes.com	GA
Lander University	landerbearcats.com	SC
University of North Georgia	saintssports.com	GA
UNC Pembroke	uncpbraves.com	NC
University South Carolina – Aiken	pacersports.com	SC
University of Montevallo	montevallofalcons.com	AL
Young Harris College	yhcathletics.com	GA

R. **Pennsylvania State Ath. Conf.** - psacsports.org

Bloomsburg University	buhuskies.com	PA
East Stroudsburg University	esuwarriors.com	PA
University of Pennsylvania - Kutztown	kubears.com	PA
Mansfield University	gomounties.com	PA
Mercyhurst University	hurstathletics.com	PA
Millersville University	millersvilleathletics.com	PA
West Chester University	wcupagoldenrams.com	PA

California University of Pennsylvania	calvulcans.com	PA
Clarion University	clariongoldeneagles.com	PA
Indiana University of Pennsylvania	iupathletics.com	PA
Lock Haven University	golhu.com	PA
Seaton Hill University	athletics.setonhill.edu	PA
Shippensburg University	shipraiders.com	PA
Slippery Rock University	rockathletics.com	PA

S.   **Rocky Mountain Ath. Conf.** - rmacsports.org

Colorado Christian University	ccucougars.com	CO
Adams State University	asugrizzlies.com	CO
CSU – Pueblo	gothunderwolves.com	CO
Colorado Mesa State University	cmumavericks.com	CO
Metro State University of Denver	gometrostate.com	CO
Colorado School of Mines	csmorediggers.com	CO
New Mexico Highlands University	nmhucowboys.com	NM
Regis University	regisrangers.com	CO

T.   **South Atlantic Conf.** - thesac.com

Brevard College	bctornados.com	NC
Carson-Newman College	cneagles.com	TN
Catawba College	gocatawbaindians.com	NC
Coker College	cokercobras.com	SC
Lenoir-Rhyne University	lrbears.com	NC
Lincoln Memorial University	lmurailsplitters.com	TN
Mars Hill College	mhclions.com	NC
Newberry College	newberrywolves.com	SC
Tusculum College	tusculumpioneers.com	TN
Wingate University	wingatebulldogs.com	NC

U.   **Southern Intercollegiate Ath. Conf.** - thesiac.com

Albany State University	asugoldenrams.com	GA
Benedict College	benedicttigers.com	SC
Claflin University	athletics.claflin.edu	SC
Clark Atlanta University	clarkatlantasports.com	GA
Morehouse College	athletics.morehouse.edu	GA
Paine College	paineathletics.com	GA
Kentucky State University	ksuthorobreds.com	KY
Lane College	golcdragons.com	TN
LeMoyne-Owen College	athletics.loc.edu	TN
Miles College	milesgoldenbears.com	AL
Stillman College	stillmanathletics.com	AL
Tuskegee University	athletics.tuskegee.edu	AL

V.   **Sunshine State Conf.** - sunshinestateconference.com

Barry University	gobarrybucs.com	FL
Eckerd College	eckerdtritons.com	FL
Florida Southern College	fscmocs.com	FL
Florida Institute of Technology	floridatechsports.com	FL
Lynn University	lynnfightingknights.com	FL
Nova Southeastern University	nsusharks.com	FL
Rollins College	rollinssports.com	FL
St. Leo University	saintleolions.com	FL
University of Tampa	tampaspartans.com	FL

W.   **West Virginia Intercollegiate Ath. Conf.** - wviac.org

Alderson-Broaddus College	gobattlers.com	WV
Davis & Elkins College	senatornation.com	WV
Fairmont State University	fightingfalcons.com	WV
West Virginia Wesleyan University	wesleyanbobcats.com	WV

Pittsburgh – Johnstown University	upj.pitt.edu	WV
Seton Hill University	athletics.setonhill.edu	WV
Shepherd University	shepardrams.com	WV
West Liberty State University	hilltoppersports.com	WV
Wheeling Jesuit University	athletics.wju.edu	WV
Glenville State College	glenville.edu/athletics.com	WV
Bluefield State College	athletics.bluefieldstate.edu	WV
University of Charleston	ucgoldeneagles.com	WV
Concord University	cumountainlions.com	WV
Ohio Valley University	ovu.edu/athletics	WV
West Virginia State University	wvsuyellowjackets.com	WV

III. NCAA Division III Baseball Colleges/Universities

CONFERENCE/   WEBSITE   STATE
SCHOOL

A. Allegheny Mountain Collegiate Conf.
amccsports.org

School	Website	State
Youville College	athletics.dyc.edu	NY
Hilbert College	hilbert.edu/athletics	NY
La Roche College	larochesports.com	PA
Medaille College	medaillesports.com	NY
Mount Aloysius College	mtaloy.edu/athletics	PA
Penn State University, Altoona	altoona.psu.edu/sports	
Pennsylvania State Univ.- Erie	psblions.com	PA
University of Pittsburgh - Bradford	athletics.pittbradford.org	PA
University of Pittsburgh - Greensburg	pittgreensburgathletics.com	PA

B. American Southwest Conf. - ascsports.org

School	Website	State
Concordia University Texas	athletics.concordia.edu	TX
East Texas Baptist University	etbusports.com	TX
Howard Payne University	hpusports.com	TX
LeTourneau University	letuathletics.com	TX
Louisiana College	lcwildcats.net	LA
University of Mary Hardin-Baylor	cruathletics.com	TX
Mississippi College	gochoctaws.com	MS
University of the Ozarks	eagles.ozarks.edu	AR
Schreiner University	testathletics.schreiner.edu	TX
Sul Ross State University	srlobos.com	TX
Texas Lutheran University	tlubulldogs.com	TX
University of Texas at Dallas	cometsports.utdallas.edu	TX

University of Texas at Tyler   uttylerpatriots.com   TX

C.   **Capital Ath. Conf.** - cacsports.com

Frostburg State University	frostburgsports.com	MD
University of Mary Washington	athletics.umw.edu	VA
Salisbury University	suseagulls.com	MD
St. Mary's College of Maryland	smcmathletics.com	MD
Wesley College	athletics.wesley.edu	DE
York College	ycp.edu/athletics	PA

D.   **Centennial Conf.** - centennial.org

Dickinson College	dickinsonathletics.com	PA
Franklin & Marshall College	godiplomats.com	PA
Gettysburg College	gettysburgsports.com	PA
Haverford College	haverfordathletics.com	PA
Johns Hopkins University	hopkinssports.com	MD
McDaniel College	mcdaniel.edu/undergraduate/athletics	MD
Muhlenberg College	muhlenberg.edu/main/athletics	PA
Swarthmore College	swarthmoreathletics.com	PA
Ursinus College	ursinusathletics.com	PA
Washington College	washcoll.edu/athletics	MD

E.   **City U. of NY Ath. Conf.** - cunyathletics.com

Baruch College	athletics.baruch.cuny.edu	NY
The City College of New York	ccny.cuny.edu/athletics	NY
John Jay College of Criminal Justice	johnjayathletics.com	NY
Lehman College	lehman.cuny.edu	NY
College of Staten Island	csidolphins.com	NY
Yeshiva University	yumacs.com	NY

108

F.   **College Conf. of IL & WI** - cciw.org

Augustana College	athletics.augustana.edu	IL
Carthage College	athletics.carthage.edu	WI
Elmhurst College	elmhurstbluejays.com	IL
Illinois Wesleyan University	iwusports.com	IL
Millikin University	athletics.millikin.edu	IL
North Central College	northcentralcardinals.com	IL
North Park University	athletics.northpark.edu	IL
Wheaton College	wheaton.edu/athletics	IL

G.   **Colonial States Ath. Conf.** - csacsports.org

Cairn University	cairnhighlanders.com	PA
Centenary College	centenarycyclones.com	NJ
Gwynedd-Mercy College	gmcgriffins.com	PA
Immaculata University	gomightymacs.com	PA
Keystone College	gokcgiants.com	PA
Marywood University	marywoodpacers.com	PA
Neumann University	neumann.edu/athletics	PA

H.   **Commonwealth Coast Conf.**
thecommonwealthcoastconference.com

Curry College	curryathletics.com	MA
Eastern Nazarene College	athletics.enc.edu	MA
Endicott College	ecgulls.com	MA
Gordon College	athletics.gordon.edu	MA
Nichols College	nicholsathletics.com	MA
Roger Williams University	rwu.edu/athletics	RI
Salve Regina University	salveathletics.com	RI
Wentworth Institute of Technology	wentworthathletics.com	MA

| Western New England University | wnegoldenbears.com | MA |

I.   **Commonwealth Conf. (MAC)** - gomacsports.com

Albright College	albrightathletics.com	PA
Alvernia University	athletics.alvernia.edu	PA
Arcadia University	athletics.arcadia.edu	PA
Elizabethtown College	etownbluejays.com	PA
Lebanon Valley College	godutchmen.com	PA
Messiah College	gomessiah.com	PA
Stevenson University	gomustangsports.com	MD
Widener University	widenerpride.com com	PA

J.   **Empire 8** - empire8.com

Elmira College	athletics.elmira.edu	NY
Houghton College	athletics.houghton.edu	NY
Ithaca College	ithaca.edu/athletics	NY
St. John Fisher College	athletics.sjfc.edu NY	
Stevens Institute of Technology	stevensducks.com	NJ
Utica College	ucpioneers.com	NY

K.   **Freedom Conf. (MAC)** - gomacsports.com

Delaware Valley College	athletics.delval.edu	PA
DeSales University	athletics.delval.edu	PA
Eastern University	goeasterneagles.com	PA
Fairleigh Dickinson University - Florham	fdudevils.com	NJ
King's College	kingscollegeathletics.com	PA
Manhattanville College	govaliants.com	NY
Misericordia University	athletics.misericordia.edu	PA
Wilkes University	gowilkesu.com	PA

110

L.   **Great Northeast Ath. Conf.** - thegnac.com

Albertus Magnus College	athletics.albertus.edu	CT
Anna Maria College	goamcats.com	MA
Emerson College	emersonlions.com	MA
Johnson and Wales	providence.jwuathletics.com	RI
- Florham		
Lasell College	lasell.edu/athletics-and-recreation	MA
Norwich University	norwichathletics.com	VT
Rivier University	rivierathletics.com	NH
Saint Joseph's College	gomonks.com	ME
Suffolk University	gosuffolkrams.com	MA

M.   **Heartland Collegiate Ath. Conf.** - Heartlandconf.org

Anderson University	athletics.anderson.edu	IN
Bluffton University	bluffton.edu/athletics	OH
Defiance College	defianceathletics.com	OH
Earlham College	goearlham.com	IN
Franklin College	franklingrizzlies.com	IN
Hanover College	hanover.edu/athletics	IN
Manchester University	muspartans.com	IN
College of Mount St. Joseph	msj.edu/athletics	OH
Rose-Hulman Institute	rose-hulman.edu/athletics	IN
of Technology		
Transylvania University	transysports.com	KY

N.   **Iowa Intercollegiate Ath. Conf.** - iowaconference.com

Buena Vista University	bvuathletics.com	IA
Central College	central.edu/athletics	IA
Coe College	coeathletics.com	IA
University of Dubuque	www.dbq.edu/athletics	IA
Loras College	duhawks.com	IA
Luther College	luther.edu/sports	IA

Simpson College	simpson.edu/athletics	IA
Wartburg College	go-knights.net	IA

O. **Landmark Conf.** - landmarkconference.org

Catholic University	cuacardinals.com	DC
Drew University	drewrangers.com	NJ
Juniata College	juniatasports.net	PA
Moravian College	moraviansports.com	PA
University of Scranton	scranton.edu/athletics	PA
Susquehanna University	gosusqu.com	PA
U.S. Merchant Marine Academy	usmma.edu/academy-life/athletics	NY

P. **Liberty League** - libertyleagueathletics.com

Clarkson University	clarksonathletics.com	NY
Rensselaer Polytechnic Institute	admissions.rpi.edu	NY
University of Rochester	rochester.edu/athletics	NY
Rochester Institute of Technology	ritathletics.com	NY
Skidmore College	skidmoreathletics.com	NY
St. Lawrence University	saintsathletics.com	NY
Union College	unionathletics.com	NY
Vassar College	vassarathletics.com	NY

Q. **Little East Conf.** - littleeast.com

Eastern Connecticut State Technology	gowarriorathletics.com	CT
Keene State College	keeneowls.com	NH
University of Massachusetts - Boston	umb.edu/athletics	MA
University of Massachusetts - Dartmouth	corsairathletics.com	MA

Plymouth State University	athletics.plymouth.edu	NH
Rhode Island College	goanchormen.com	RI
University of Southern Maine	usm.maine.edu	ME
Western Connecticut State University	wcsuathletics.com	CT

R. **MA State Collegiate Ath. Conf.** - mascac.com

Bridgewater State University	bsubears.com	MA
Fitchburg State University	fitchburgfalcons.com	MA
Framingham State University	fsurams.com	MA
Massachusetts College of Liberal Arts	athletics.mcla.edu	MA
Massachusetts Maritime Academy	mmabucs.com	MA
Salem State University	salemstatevikings.com	MA
Westfield State University	westfieldstateowls.com	MA
Worcester State University	wsulancers.com	MA

S. **Michigan Intercollegiate Ath. Assn.** - miaa.org

Adrian College .	adrianbulldogs.com	MI
Albion College	albion.edu/athletics	MI
Alma College	goalmascots.com	MI
Calvin College	calvin.edu/community/sports	MI
Hope College	athletics.hope.edu	MI
Kalamazoo College	hornets.kzoo.edu	MI
Olivet College	olivetcomets.com	MI
Trine University	trine.edu/athletics	IN

T. **Midwest Conf.** - midwestconference.org

| Beloit College | beloit.edu/bucs | WI |
| Carroll University | carroll.edu/athletics | WI |

Cornell College	cornellrams.com	IA
Grinnell College	pioneers.grinnell.edu	IA
Illinois College	illinoiscollegeathletics.com	IL
Knox College	prairiefire.knox.edu	IL
Lawrence University	lawrence.edu/athletics	WI
Monmouth College	monmouthscots.com	IL
Ripon College	redhawks.ripon.edu	WI
St. Norbert College	snc.edu/athletics	WI

U.   **Minnesota Intercollegiate Ath. Conf.** - miacathletics.com

Augsburg College	athletics.augsburg.edu	MN
Bethel University	athletics.bethel.edu	MN
Carleton College	carleton.edu/athletics	MN
Concordia College - Moorhead	concordiamn.prestosports.com	MN
Gustavus Adolphus College	gustavus.edu/athletics	MN
Hamline University	hamlineathletics.com	MN
Macalester College	athletics.macalester.edu	MN
St. John's University	gojohnnies.com	MN
Saint Mary's University of Minnesota	saintmaryssports.com	MN
St. Olaf College	stolaf.edu/athletics	MN
University of St. Thomas	stthomas.edu/athletics	MN

V.   **New England Collegiate Conf.** - neccathletics.com

Becker College	beckerhawks.com	MA
Daniel Webster College	athletics.dwc.edu	NH
Elms College	elms.edu/elms-athletics	MA
Lesley University	athletics.lesley.edu	MA
Mitchell College	mitchellathletics.com	CT
Newbury College	newburynighthawks.com	MA
Southern Vermont College	svcathletics.com	VT

W.   New England Small College Ath. Conf. - nescac.com

Amherst College	amherst.edu/athletics	MA
Bates College	athletics.bates.edu	ME
Bowdoin College	athletics.bowdoin.edu	ME
Colby College	colby.edu/athletics	ME
Hamilton College	hamilton.edu/athletics	NY
Middlebury College	middlebury.edu/athletics	VT
Trinity College	athletics.trincoll.edu	CT
Tufts University	gotuftsjumbos.com	MA
Wesleyan University	wesleyan.edu/athletics	CT
Williams College	athletics.williams.edu	MA

X.   New England Women's and Men's Ath. Conf.
newmacsports.com

Babson College	babsonathletics.com	MA
Clark University	clarkathletics.com	MA
Emerson College	emersonlions.com	MA
Massachusetts Institute of Technology	mitathletics.com	MA
Springfield College	spfldcol.edu/homepage/athletics	MA
U.S. Coast Guard Academy	uscgasports.com	CT
Wheaton College	athletics.wheaton.edu	MA
Worcester Polytechnic Institute	wpi.prestosports.com	MA

Y.   New Jersey Ath. Conf. - njacsports.com

Kean University	keanathletics.com	NJ
Montclair State University	montclairathletics.com	NJ
New Jersey City University	njcugothicknights.com	NJ
The College of New Jersey	tcnjathletics.com	NJ
Ramapo College	ramapoathletics.com	NJ
Richard Stockton College of New Jersey	stocktonathletics.com	NJ

Rowan University	rowanathletics.com	NJ
State Univ. of New Jersey - Camden	athletics.camden.rutgers.edu	NJ
State Univ. of New Jersey - Newark	rutgersnewarkathletics.com	NJ
William Paterson University of New Jersey	wpupioneers.com	NJ

Z.   North Atlantic Conf. - nacathletics.com

Castleton State College	castletonsports.com	VT
Colby-Sawyer College	colby-sawyerathletics.com	NH
Husson University	athletics.husson.edu	ME
University of Maine - Farmington	athletics.umf.maine.edu	ME
Lyndon State College	lyndonhornets.com	VT
New England College	athletics.nec.edu	NH
Thomas College	athletics.thomas.edu	ME

AA.   North Coast Athletic Conf. - northcoast.org

Allegheny College	alleghenysports.com	PA
Denison University	denisonbigred.com	OH
DePauw University	depauw.edu/athletics	IN
Hiram College	hiramterriers.com	OH
Kenyon College	athletics.kenyon.edu	OH
Oberlin College	goyeo.com	OH
Ohio Wesleyan University	battlingbishops.com	OH
Wabash College	sports.wabash.edu	IN
Wittenberg University	wittenbergtigers.com	OH
College of Wooster	woosterathletics.com	OH

BB.   North Eastern Ath. Conf. - Neacsports.com

Bryn Athyn College	brynathynathletics.com	PA

Cazenovia College	cazenoviawildcats.com	NY
Gallaudet University	gallaudetathletics.com	DC
Keuka College	keukastorm.com	NY
Lancaster Bible College	lbcchargers.com	PA
Penn College of Technology	pct.edu/athletics	PA
Penn State Berks	psuberksathletics.com	PA
Penn State Abington	abingtonsports.com	PA
SUNY- IT	wildcats.sunyit.edu	NY

CC. **Northern Ath. Conf.** - naccsports.org

Aurora University	athletics.aurora.edu	IL
Benedictine University	benueagles.com	IL
Concordia University	cuwfalcons.com	WI
Concordia University Chicago	cucougars.com	IL
Dominican University	dustars.com	IL
Edgewood College	edgewoodcollegeeagles.com	WI
Lakeland College	lakelandmuskies.com	WI
Maranatha Baptist Bible College	sabreathletics.com	WI
Marian University	muknights.com	WI
Milwaukee School of Engineering	go-raiders.com	WI
Rockford University	goregents.com	IL
Wisconsin Lutheran College	wlcsports.com	WI

DD. **Northwest Conf.** - nwcsports.com

George Fox University	athletics.georgefox.edu	OR
Lewis & Clark College	lcpioneers.com	OR
Linfield College	linfield.edu/sports	OR
Pacific Lutheran University	golutes.com	WA
Pacific University (Oregon)	goboxers.com	OR
University of Puget Sound	loggerathletics.com	WA
Whitman College	athletics.whitman.edu	WA
Whitworth University	whitworthpirates.com	WA

Willamette University   willamette.edu/athletics   OR

EE.   **Ohio Ath. Conf.** - oac.org

Baldwin Wallace University	bwyellowjackets.com	OH
Capital University	athletics.capital.edu	OH
Heidelberg University	heidelberg.edu/athletics	OH
John Carroll University	jcusports.com	OH
Marietta College	pioneers.marietta.edu	OH
University of Mount Union	athletics.mountunion.edu	OH
Muskingum University	muskingum.edu	OH
Ohio Northern University	onusports.com	OH
Otterbein University	otterbeincardinals.com	OH
Wilmington College	wilmingtonquakers.com	OH

FF.   **Old Dominion Ath. Conf.** - odaconline.com

Bridgewater College	bridgewatereagles.com	VA
Eastern Mennonite University	emuroyals.com	VA
Emory and Henry College	gowasps.com	VA
Guilford College	guilfordquakers.com	NC
Hampden-Sydney College	hscathletics.com	VA
Lynchburg College	athletics.lynchburg.edu	VA
Roanoke College	maroons.roanoke.edu	VA
Shenandoah University	suhornets.com	VA
Virginia Wesleyan College	vwcathletics.com	VA
Washington and Lee University	generalssports.com	VA

GG.   **Presidents' Ath. Conf.** - pacathletics.org

Bethany College	bethanywv.edu/athletics	WV
Geneva College	geneva.edu/page/msports	PA
Grove City College	gcc.edu/sports	PA
Saint Vincent College	athletics.stvincent.edu	PA
Thiel College	thielathletics.com	PA

Thomas More College	tmcsaints.com	KY
Washington and Jefferson College	washjeff.edu/athletics	PA
Waynesburg University	waynesburgsports.com	PA
Westminster College	wcbluejays.com	PA

HH.   **Skyline Conf.** - skylineconference.org

State University of NY Farmingdale	farmingdalesports.com	NY
State University of NY Maritime	maritimeathletics.com	NY
Mount Saint Mary College	msmcknights.com	NY
College of Mount St. Vincent	cmsvathletics.com	NY
State University College at Old Westbury	oldwestburypanthers.com	NY
Polytechnic Institute of New York U.	gonyupoly.com	NY
Purchase College State U. of New York	purchasecollegeathletics.com	NY
St. Joseph's College	sjceagles.com	NY
Yeshiva University	yumacs.com	NY
The Sages Colleges	sagegators.com	NY

II.   **Southern Ath. Assoc.** - saa-sports.com

Berry College	berryvikings.com	GA
Birmingham-Southern College	bscsports.net	AL
Centre College	centreathletics.com	KY
Hendrix College	hendrixwarriors.com	AR
Millsaps College	gomajors.com	MS
Oglethorpe University	gopetrels.com	GA
Rhodes College	rhodeslynx.com	TN

University of the South   sewaneetigers.com   TN

JJ.   Southern California Intercollegiate Ath. Conf.
thesciac.org

California Institute of Technology	gocaltech.com	CA
California Lutheran University	clusports.com	CA
Chapman University	chapmanathletics.com	CA
Claremont McKenna Harvey Mudd, Scripps Colleges (unified)	cmsathletics.org	CA
University of La Verne	leopardathletics.com	CA
Occidental College	oxyathletics.com	CA
Pomona-Pitzer Colleges	pe.pomona.edu	CA
University of Redlands	goredlands.com	CA
Whittier College	wcpoets.com	CA

KK.   Southern Collegiate Ath. Conf. - scacsports.com

Austin College	acroos.com	TX
Centenary College	gocentenary.com	LA
University of Dallas	udallasathletics.com	TX
Southwestern University	southwesternpirates.com	TX
Trinity University	trinitytigers.com	TX

LL.   St. Louis Intercollegiate Ath. Conf. - sliac.org

Blackburn College	blackburnbeavers.com	IL
Eureka College	eurekareddevils.com	IL
Fontbonne University	fontbonnegriffins.com	MO
Greenville College	greenville.edu/athletics	IL
MacMurray College	mac.edu/athletics	IL
Principia College	principiaathletics.com	IL
Spalding University	spaldingathletics.com	KY

| Webster University | websterathletics.com | MO |
| Westminster College | westminster-mo.edu/athletics | MO |

MM. **St. Univ. of NY Ath. Conf.** - sunyac.com

State University of New York - Brockport	gobrockport.com	NY
State University of New York - Cortland	cortlandreddragons.com	NY
State University College - Fredonia	fredoniabluedevils.com	NY
State University College - New Paltz	nphawks.com	NY
State University College - Oneonta	oneontaathletics.com	NY
State University of New York - Oswego	athletics.oswego.edu	NY
Plattsburgh State	gocardinalsports.com	NY

NN. **USA South Ath. Conf.** - usasouth.net

Averett University	averettcougars.com	VA
Covenant College	athletics.covenant.edu	GA
Ferrum College	ferrumpanthers.com	VA
Greensboro College	greensborocollegesports.com	NC
Huntington College	huntingdonhawks.com	AL
La Grange College	lagrangepanthers.com	GA
Maryville College	mcscots.com	TN
Mary Baldwin College	mbcathletics.com	VA
Methodist University	mumonarchs.com	NC
North Carolina Wesleyan College II	ncwcsports.com	NC
Piedmont College	piedmontlions.com	GA
William Peace University	gopeacepacers.org	NC

OO. **University Ath. Assoc.** - uaasports.info

Brandeis University	brandeisjudges.com	MA
Case Western Reserve University	athletics.case.edu	OH
University of Chicago	athletics.uchicago.edu	IL
Emory University	emoryathletics.com	GA
University of Rochester	rochester.edu/athletics	NY
Washington University	wustl.edu/athletics	MO

PP. **Upper Midwest Ath. Conf.** - umacathletics.com

Bethany Lutheran College	blcvikings.com	MN
Crown College	athletics.crown.edu	MN
Martin Luther College	mlc-wels.edu/home/athletics	MN
University of Minnesota Morris	ummcougars.org	MN
North Central University	ncurams.com	MN
Northland College	northlandcollegesports.com	WI
Northwestern College	nwceagles.com	MN
The College of St. Scholastica	csssaints.com	MN

QQ. **Western Ath. Conf.** - wacsports.com

Bakersfield College	gorunners.com	CA
Chicago State	gocsucougars.com	IL
Grand Canyon College	gculopes.com	NV
New Mexico State	nmstatesports.com	NM
Seattle University	goseattleu.com	WA
Texas-Pan American	utpabroncs.com	TX
Utah Valley University	wolverinegreen.com	UT

RR. **Wisconsin Intercollegiate Ath. Conf.** - wiacsports.com

University of Wisconsin - La Crosse	uwlathletics.com	WI

University of Wisconsin - Oshkosh	uwoshkoshtitans.com	WI
University of Wisconsin - Platteville	athletics.uwplatt.edu	WI
University of Wisconsin - Stevens Point	athletics.uwsp.edu	WI
University of Wisconsin - Stout	uwstout.edu	WI
University of Wisconsin - Superior	uwsyellowjackets.com	WI
University of Wisconsin - Whitewater	uwwsports.com	WI

IV. National Assoc. of Intercollegiate Athletics (NAIA)
Baseball Colleges/Universities - naia.org

CONFERENCE/ SCHOOL	WEBSITE	STATE

A. Assoc. of Independent Institutions - aiisports.com

Ashford University	ashfordathletics.com	IA
University of Antelope Valley	uavpioneers.com	CA
University of British Columbia	gothunderbirds.ca	BC
California State University - San Marcos	csusm.edu/athletics	CA
Fisher College	fisherfalcons.com	MA
Georgia Gwinnett College	grizzlyathletics.com	GA
University of Houston - Victoria	uhvjaguars.com	TX
Lindenwood University	lindenwoodlynx.com	IL
Louisiana State University - Alexandria	athletics.lsua.edu	LA
Morris College	morris.edu/athletics	SC
West Virginia University- IT	goldenbearathletics.com	WV

B. American Midwest Conf. - amcsportsonline.com

Benedictine University at Springfield	benubulldogs.com	IL
Freed-Hardeman University	gofhulions.com	TN
Hannibal-LaGrange University	hlgtrojans.com	MO
Harris-Stowe State University	hornetsathletics.com	MO
Lyon College	lyonscots.com	AR
Mid Continent University	midcontinentcougars.com	KY
Missouri Baptist University	mbuspartans.com	MO
Park University	parkathletics.com	MO
Stephens College	stephens.edu/athletics	MO

Williams Baptist College   wbceagles.com   AR

C.   **Appalachian Ath. Conf.** - aacsports.com

Bryan College	bryanlions.com	TN
Milligan College	milliganbuffs.com	TN
Montreat College	montreatcavaliers.com	NC
Point University	pointskyhawks.com	GA
Reinhardt University	reinhardteagles.com	GA
St. Andrews University	sauknights.com	NC
Tennessee Wesleyan College	twcbulldogs.com	TN
Truett-McConnell College	tmcbears.com	GA
Union College	ucbulldogs.com	KY

D.   **Cascade Collegiate Conf.** - cascadeconference.org

Concordia University	gocugo.com	OR
Corban University	gowarriorsgo.com	OR
The College of Idaho	yoteathletics.com	ID
Oregon Institute of Technology	oitsports.com	OR

E.   **Chicagoland Collegiate Ath. Conf.** - ccacsports.com

Calumet College of St. Joseph	ccsj.edu/athletics	IN
Holy Cross College	hcsaints.com	IN
Robert Morris University	rmueagles.com	IL
Roosevelt University	rooseveltlakers.com	IL
University of St. Francis	gofightingsaints.com	IL
Saint Xavier University	sxucougars.com	IL
Trinity Christian College	athletics.trnty.edu	IL
Trinity International University	tiutrojans.com	IL

F.   **Crossroads League** - crossroadsleague.com

Bethel College	bethelcollegepilots.com	IN
Goshen College	goleafs.net	IN
Grace College	gclancers.com	IN
Huntington University	huntington.edu/athletics	IN
Indiana Wesleyan University	iwuwildcats.com	IN
Marian University	muknights.com	IN
Mount Vernon Nazarene University	mvnucougars.com	OH
University of Saint Francis	saintfranciscougars.com	IN
Spring Arbor University	saucougars.com	MI
Taylor University	athletics.taylor.edu	IN

G.   **Gulf Coast Ath. Conf.** - gcaconf.com

Talladega College	talladegatornadoes.com	AL
Tougaloo College	tougaloobulldogs.com	MS
Edward Waters College	ewc.edu	FL
Voorhees College	voorhees.edu/athletics	SC

H.   **Great Plains Ath. Conf.** - gpacsports.com

Briar Cliff University	bcuchargers.com	IA
Concordia University	cune.edu/athletics	NE
Dakota Wesleyan University	dwuathletics.com	SD
Doane College	doane.edu/Athletics	NE
Dordt College	dordt.edu/athletics	IA
Hastings College	hastingsbroncos.com	NE
Midland University	midlandathletics.com	NE
Morningside College	morningside.edu	IA
Mount Marty College	mtmc.edu/athletics	SD
Nebraska Wesleyan University	nwusports.com	NE
Northwestern College	nwcraiders.com	IA

I. **Golden State Ath. Conf.** - gsacsports.org

Arizona Christian University	acufirestorm.com	AZ
Biola University	athletics.biola.edu	CA
Concordia University	cuieagles.com	CA
The Master's College	masters.edu/athletics	CA
San Diego Christian College	sdcchawks.com	CA
Vanguard University	vanguardlions.com	CA
Westmont College	westmont.edu/athletics	CA

J. **Heart of America Ath. Conf.** - haacsports.com

Avila University	avila.edu/athletics	MO
Baker University	www.bakeru.edu/athletics	KS
Benedictine College	ravenathletics.com	KS
Central Methodist University	athletics.centralmethodist.edu	MO
Culver-Stockton College	cscwildcats.com	MO
Evangel University	evangel.edu/athletics	MO
Graceland University	gujackets.com	IA
MidAmerica Nazarene University	mnusports.com	KS
Missouri Valley College	moval.edu/athletics	MO
Peru State College	pscbobcats.com	NE

K. **Kansas Collegiate Ath. Conf.** - kcacsports.com

Bethany College	bethanyswedes.com	KS
Friends University	friendsathletics.com	KS
Kansas Wesleyan University	kwucoyotes.com	KS
McPherson College	macbulldogs.com	KS
Ottawa University	ottawabraves.com	KS
University of Saint Mary	gospires.com	KS
Sterling College	scwarriors.com	KS
Tabor College	taborbluejays.com	KS

L.   Kentucky Intercollegiate Ath. Conf. - kiacsports.com

Alice Lloyd College	alc.edu/athletics	KY
Asbury University	asbury.edu/athletics	KY
Berea College	bereaathletics.com	KY
Brescia University	brescia.edu/athletics	KY
Indiana University Southeast	iusathletics.com	IN
Point Park University	pointpark.edu/athletics	PA

M.   Midlands Collegiate Ath. Conf. - mcac-naia.org

Bellevue University	bubruins.com	NE
Central Baptist College	cbcmustangs.com	AR
Central Christian College	ccctigers.com	KS
College of Saint Mary	csmflames.com	NE
Oklahoma Wesleyan University	okwu.edu/athletics	OK
College of the Ozarks	cofo.edu/athletics	MO
Waldorf College	waldorfwarriors.com	IA
York College	ycpanthers.com	NE

N.   Midwest Collegiate Conf.
midwestcollegiateconference.com

AIB College of Business	aib-eagles.com	IA
Clarke University	clarkecrusaders.com	IA
Grand View University	gvvikings.com	IA
Mount Mercy University	mountmercymustangs.com	IA
Saint Ambrose University	sau.edu/athletics	IA
Viterbo University	viterboathletics.com	WI
William Penn University	statesmenathletics.com	IA

O.   Mid-South Conf. - mid-southconference.org

Bluefield College	bluefield.edu/athletics	VA
Campbellsville University	campbellsvilletigers.com	KY

Cumberland University	gocumberlandathletics.com	TN
University of the Cumberlands	cumberlandspatriots.com	KY
Georgetown College	georgetowncollegeathletics.com	KY
Lindsey Wilson College	lindseyathletics.com	KY
University of Pikeville	upikebears.com	KY
University of Rio Grande	rioredstorm.com	OH
St. Catharine College	goscpatriots.com	KY
Shawnee State University	ssubears.com	OH

P.   **Red River Athletic Conf.** - redriverconference.com

Bacone College	athletics.bacone.edu	OK
Huston-Tillotson University	athletics.htu.edu	TX
Jarvis Christian College	jarvis.edu	TX
Langston University	langstonsports.com	OK
Louisiana State University Shreveport	lsus.edu/athletics	LA
University of the Southwest	uswmustangs.com	NM
Texas College	texascollege.edu/athletics	TX
Wiley College	wileyc.edu/athletics	TX

Q.   **Sooner Ath. Conf.** - soonerathletic.org

Mid-America Christian University	macuathletics.cstv.com	OK
Northwood University	knights.gonorthwood.com	TX
Oklahoma Baptist University	obubison.com	OK
Oklahoma City University	ocusports.com	OK
Southwestern Assemblies of God Univ.	sagu.edu/athletics	OK
Southwestern Christian University	scueagles.com	OK
Texas Wesleyan University	ramsports.net	TX
Saint Gregory's University	sgucavaliers.com	OK

University of Science and Arts of Oklahoma	usao.edu/sports	OK
Wayland Baptist University	wbuathletics.com	TX

R.   **Southern States Ath. Conf.** - ssacsports.com

Auburn University Montgomery	aumathletics.com	AL
Belhaven University	blazers.belhaven.edu	MS
Bethel University	bethelathletics.com	TN
Blue Mountain College	bmcsports.com	MS
Brenau University	brenautigers.com	GA
Brewton-Parker College	gobaronsgo.com	GA
Emmanuel College	goeclions.com	GA
Faulkner University	faulknereagles.com	AL
Loyola University	wolfpack.loyno.edu	LA
Martin Methodist College	goredhawks.com	TN
University of Mobile	umobile.edu/athletic	AL
Southern Polytechnic State University	spsuhornets.com	GA
Southern Wesleyan University	swuathletics.com	SC
Spring Hill College	shcbadgers.com	AL
William Carey University	careyathletics.com	MS

S.   **The Sun Conf.**   thesunconference.com

Ave Maria University	avemariagyrenes.com	FL
Embry-Riddle Aeronautical University	erauathletics.com	FL
Florida Memorial University	fmuathletics.com	FL
Northwood University	seahawks.gonorthwood.com	FL
Saint Thomas University	stubobcats.com	FL
University of South Carolina - Beaufort	uscbathletics.com	SC
Southeastern University	seufire.com	FL
Thomas University	thomasu.edu/athletics	GA

| Warner University | warnerroyals.com | FL |
| Webber International University | webberathletics.com | FL |

T. **Wolverine-Hoosier Ath. Conf.** - whac.net

Aquinas College	aquinas.edu/athletics	MI
Concordia University	concordiacardinals.com	MI
Cornerstone University	cugoldeneagles.com	MI
Davenport University	dupanthers.com	MI
Indiana Institute of Technology	indianatech.edu/athletics	IN
Lourdes University	lourdesathletics.com	OH
Madonna University	madonnacrusaders.com	MI
University of Northwestern Ohio	unohracers.com	OH
Siena Heights University	shusaints.com	OH
University of Michigan - Dearborn	gowolves.net	MI

V. National Junior College Ath. Assoc. (NJCAA) Baseball Colleges - njcaa.org

CONFERENCE   WEBSITE
SCHOOL/CITY/ STATE

A. Alabama Comm. College Conf. - Region 17
acccathletics.com

School/City State	Website
Alabama Southern Comm. College Monroeville AL	ascc.edu
Bishop State Comm. College Mobile AL	bishop.edu/athletics
Calhoun Comm. College Decatur AL	calhoun.edu
Central Alabama Comm. College Alexander City AL	cacc.edu
Chattahoochee Valley Com. College Phenix City AL	athletics.cv.edu
Enterprise State Comm. College Enterprise AL	escc.edu
Gadsden State Comm. College Gadsden AL	gadsdenstate.edu
Faulkner State Comm. College Bay Minette AL	faulknerstate.edu
Jefferson Davis Comm. College Brewton AL	warhawks.jdcc.edu
Lawson State Comm. College Bessemer AL	ls.cc.al.us
Lurleen B. Wallace Comm. College Andalusia AL	lbwcc.edu
Marion Military Institute Marion AL	marionmilitary.edu
Shelton State Comm. College Tuscaloosa AL	sheltonstate.edu

Snead State Comm. College   snead.edu
    Sand Mountain AL
Southern Union State Comm. College   suscc.edu
    Wadley AL
Wallace State Comm. College   wallace.edu
    Dothan AL

B.   **Arizona Comm. College Athletic Conf. - Region 1**
    accac.org

Arizona Western College   azwestern.edu
    Yuma AZ
Central Arizona College   centralaz.edu
    Coolidge AZ
Chandler-Gilbert Comm. College   cgc.maricopa.edu
    Chandler AZ
Cochise College   goapaches.com
    Douglas AZ
Eastern Arizona College   eacmonsters.com
    Thatcher AZ
GateWay Comm. College   gatewaycc.edu
    Phoenix AZ
Glendale Comm. College   gccaz.edu
    Glendale AZ
Mesa Comm. College   mesacc.edu
    Mesa AZ
Paradise Valley Comm. College   pvc.maricopa.edu
    Phoenix AZ
Phoenix College   phoenixcollege.edu
    Phoenix AZ
Pima Comm. College   pima.edu
    Tucson AZ
Scottsdale Comm. College   scottsdalecc.edu
    Scottsdale AZ

South Mountain Comm. College   southmountaincc.edu
    Phoenix AZ
Yavapai College   goroughriders.com
    Prescott AZ

C.   **Arrowhead Conf. - Region 4**

Black Hawk College   bhc.edu/athletics
    Moline IL
Carl Sandburg College   sandburg.edu
    Galesburg IL
Highland Comm. College   highland.edu/athletics
    Freeport IL
Illinois Valley Comm. College   ivcc.edu/athletics
    Oglesby IL
Kishwaukee College   kishwaukeecollege.edu
    Malta IL
Sauk Valley Comm. College.   svcc.edu
    Dixon IL

D.   **Bi-State Ath. Conf. - Region 2**

Arkansas Baptist College   arkansasbaptist.edu
    Little Rock AR
Carl Albert State College   carlalbert.edu
    Poteau OK
Connors State College   connorsstate.edu
    Warner OK
Murray State College   mscok.edu
    Tishomingo OK.
Eastern Oklahoma State College   eosc.edu
    Wilburton OK
North Arkansas College   northark.edu
    Harrison AR

Northeastern Oklahoma A&M College	neo.edu
Miami OK	
Northern Oklahoma College	noc.edu
Enid OK	
Northern Oklahoma College	noc.edu
Tonkawa OK	
Redlands Comm. College	redlandscc.edu
El Reno OK	
Rose State College	rose.edu/athletics
Midwest City OK	
Seminole State College	sscathletics.com
Seminole OK	
Western Oklahoma State College	wosc.edu
Altus OK	

E.   **Carolinas Junior College Ath. Assoc. - Region 10**

Aiken Technical College	www.atc.edu
Graniteville SC	
Blue Ridge Comm. College	blueridge.edu
Flat Rock NC	
Brunswick Comm. College	brunswickcc.edu
Supply NC	
Catawba Valley Comm. College	gocvcc.com
Hickory NC	
Central Virginia Comm. College	cvcc.vccs.edu/athletics
Lynchburg VA	
College of Albamarle	albemarle.edu
Elizabeth City NC	
Florence–Darlington Technical College	fdtc.edu
Florence SC	
Guilford Technical Comm. College	gtcc.edu
Jamestown SC	
Lenoir Comm. College	lenoircc.edu
Kinston NC	

Louisburg College	louisburg.edu
Louisburg NC	
Patrick Henry Comm. College	athletics.patrickhenry.edu
Martinsville VA	
Pitt Comm. College	pitt.edu
Winterville NC	
Rockingham Comm. College	www.rockinghamcc.edu
Wentworth NC	
Southeastern Comm. College	sccnc.edu
Whiteville NC	
Spartanburg Methodist College	gosmcpioneers.com
Spartanburg SC	
Surry Comm. College	surry.edu
Dobson NC	
USC -Lancaster	usclancaster.sc.edu
Lancaster SC	
USC- Salkehatchie	uscsalkehatchie.sc.edu
Allendale SC	
USC Sumter	uscsumter.edu
Sumter SC	
Wake Technical Comm. College	waketech.edu
Raleigh NC	

F.   **Iowa Comm. College Athletic Conf. Region 11**
iccac.org

Des Moines Area Comm. College	dmacc.edu/athletics
Boone IA	
Ellsworth Comm. College	ellsworth.edu
Iowa Falls IA	
Indian Hills Comm. College-	indianhillsathletics.com
Centerville IA	

Indian Hills Comm. College	indianhills.edu
Ottumwa IA	
Iowa Central Comm. College	iowacentral.edu
Fort Dodge IA	
Iowa Lakes Comm. College	iowalakes.edu
Estherville IA	
Iowa Western Comm. College	athletics.iwcc.edu
Council Bluffs IA	
Kirkwood Comm. College	kirkwood.edu
Cedar Rapids IA	
Marshalltown Comm. College	iavalley.edu
Marshalltown IA	
Muscatine Comm. College	
Muscatine IA	eicc.edu/athletics
North Iowa Area Comm. College	
Mason City IA	niacctrojans.com
Southeastern Comm. College	
West Burlington IA	tinyurl.com
Southwestern Comm. College	
Creston IA	swcciowa.edu

G. **Florida College System Activities Assoc.-Region 8**
thefcsaa.com/athletics

Broward College	broward.edu
Davie FL	
Chipola College	chipolaathletics.com
Marianna FL	
College of Central Florida	cf.edu
Ocala FL	
Daytona State College	daytonastate.edu
Daytona Beach FL	
Eastern Florida State College	easternflorida.edu/athletics
Melbourne FL	

Florida State College	gobluewave.com
Jacksonville FL	
Gulf Coast State College	gulfcoast.edu
Panama City FL	
Hillsborough Comm. College	hccfl.edu
Tampa FL	
Indian River State College	www.irsc.edu/athletics/athletics.aspx
Ft. Pierce FL	
Lake-Sumter State College	lssc.edu
Leesburg FL	
Miami Dade College	mdc.edu
Miami FL	
Northwest Florida State College	nwfsc.edu
Niceville FL	
Palm Beach State College	palmbeachstate.edu
Lake Worth FL	
Pasco-Hernando Comm. College	phsc.edu/athletics
New Port Richey FL	
Pensacola State College	pensacolastate.edu
Pensacola FL	
Polk State College	polk.edu
Winter Haven FL	
Santa Fe College	sfcollege.edu
Gainesville FL	
Seminole State College of Florida	seminolestate.edu
Sanford FL	
South Florida State College	southflorida.edu
Avon Park FL	
St. Johns River State College	sjrstate.edu
Palatka FL	
St. Petersburg College	spcollege.edu
St. Petersburg FL	
State College of Florida	scfmanatees.com
Bradenton FL	

Tallahassee Comm. College   tcceagles.com
        Tallahassee FL

H.   Garden State Ath. Conf. - Region 19

Atlantic Cape Comm. College   atlantic.edu
        Mays Landing NJ
Bergen Comm. College   bergen.edu
        Paramus NJ
Brookdale Comm. College   brookdalecc.edu
        Lincroft NJ
Burlington Comm. College   bcc.edu
        Pemberton NJ
Camden County College   camdencc.edu/athletics
        Blackwood NJ
County College of Morris   ccm.edu
        Randolph NJ
Cumberland County College   cccnj.edu
        Vineland NJ
Gloucester County College   gccnj.edu
        Sewell NJ
Mercer County Comm. College   mercer.edu
        Trenton NJ
Middlesex County College   middlesexcc.edu
        Edison NJ
Ocean County College   ocean.edu
        Toms River NJ
Raritan Valley Comm. College   raritanval.edu
        Branchburg NJ
Salem Comm. College   salemcc.edu
        Carney's Point NJ
Sussex County Comm. College   sussex.edu
        Newtown NJ
Union County College   ucc.edu
        Cranford NJ

I.   **NJCAA- Region 19** - region19.org

Bucks County Comm. College	bucks.edu
Newtown PA	
Delaware County Comm. College	dccc.edu
Media PA	
Delaware Technical Comm. College	dtcc.edu
Georgetown DE	
Lackawanna College	lackawanna.edu
Scranton PA	
Lehigh Carbon Comm. College	lcc.edu
Schneckville PA	
Luzerne County Comm. College	luzerne.edu
Nanticoke PA	
Montgomery County Comm. College	mc3.edu
Blue Bell PA	
Northampton Comm. College	nccspartans.com
Bethlehem PA	

J.   **NJCAA- Region 20**

Butler County Comm. College	bc3.edu
Butler PA	
Comm. College of Allegheny County	ccac.edu
West Mifflin PA	
Potomac State	potomacstatecollege.edu
Keyser WV	
Westmoreland County Comm. College	wccc.edu
Youngwood PA	

K. NJCAA - Region 9 - region9athletics.com

Lamar Comm. College Lamar CO	lamarcc.edu/athletics
McCook Comm. College McCook NE	mpcc.edu
Northeastern Junior College Sterling CO	njc.edu/athletics
Otero Junior College La Junta CO	www.ojc.edu/athletics
Trinidad State Junior College Trinidad CO	trinidadstate.edu
Western Nebraska Comm. College Scottsbluff NE	wncc.edu

L. **Georgia College Ath. Assoc. - Region 17**
thegcaa.com

Abraham Baldwin Agricultural College Tifton GA	abac.edu/athletics
Andrew College Cuthbert GA	andrewcollege.edu
Darton State College Albany GA	cavs.darton.edu
East Georgia State College Swainsboro GA	ega.edu/athletics
Georgia Highlands College Rome GA	highlands.edu/athletics
Georgia Military College Milledgeville GA	athletics.gmc.cc.ga.us
Georgia Perimeter College Decatur GA	gpc.edu
Gordon State College Barnesville GA	gordonstate.edu

Middle Georgia State College   mga.edu
    Cochran GA
South Georgia State College   sgsc.edu
    Douglas GA

M.   **Great Rivers Ath. Conf. -Region 24 -** gracsports.com

John A. Logan College   jalc.edu/athletics
    Carterville IL
Kaskaskia College   kaskaskia.edu/athletics
    Centralia IL
Lake Land College   lakeland.cc.il.us
    Mattoon IL
Lincoln Trail College   ltcathletics.com
    Robinson IL
Olney Central College   olneycentralathletics.com
    Olney IL
Rend Lake College   rlc.edu/warriors
    Ina IL
Southeastern Illinois College   sic.edu/athletics
    Harrisburg IL
Southwestern Illinois College   swic.edu/athletics
    Belleville IL
Wabash Valley College   wvcwarriorathletics.com
    Mt. Carmel IL

N.   **Illinois N4C Conf. Region 4**
    n4csports.com

College of DuPage   cod.edu
    Glen Ellyn IL
Joliet Junior College   jjc.edu
    Joliet IL

Kankakee Comm. College   kcc.edu/athletics
    Kankakee IL
Madison College   madisoncollegeathletics.com
    Madison WI
Milwaukee Area Technical College   matc.edu
    Milwaukee WI
Olive-Harvey College   oliveharvey.ccc.edu
    Chicago IL
Rock Valley College   rockvalleycollege.edu
    Rockford IL
South Suburban College   ssc.edu
    South Holland IL
Triton College   triton.edu
    River Grove IL
William Rainey Harper College   harperhawks.net
    Palatine IL

O.   Illinois Skyway Conf. - Region 4

College of Lake County   clcillinois.edu
    Grayslake IL
Elgin Comm. College   elgin.edu
    Elgin IL
McHenry County College   mchenry.edu
    Crystal Lake IL
Moraine Valley Comm. College   morainevalley.edu
    Palos Hills IL
Morton College   morton.edu
    Cicero IL
Oakton Comm. College   oakton.edu
    Des Plaines IL
Prairie State College   prairiestate.edu
    Chicago Heights IL
Waubonsee Comm. College   waubonsee.edu
    Sugar Grove IL

P. **Kansas Jayhawk Comm. College Conf. - Region 6**
kjccc.org

1. Eastern Division

Allen Comm. College Iola KS	allencc.edu
Coffeyville Comm. College Coffeyville KS	coffeyville.edu
Cowley College Arkansas City KS	cowley.edu
Fort Scott Comm. College Fort Scott KS	fsgreyhounds.com
Highland Comm. College Highland KS	highlandcc.edu
Independence Comm. College Independence KS	indycc.edu
Johnson County Comm. College Overland Park KS	jccc.edu/cavs
Kansas City Kansas Comm. College Kansas City KS	kckcc.edu
Labette Comm. College Parsons KS	labette.edu
Neosho County Comm. College Chanute KS	goneosho.com

2. Western Division

Barton Comm. College Great Bend KS	bartonSports.com
Butler Comm. College El Dorado KS	butlergrizzlies.com
Cloud County Comm. College Concordia KS	cloud.edu

Colby Comm. College Colby KS	www.colbycc.edu
Dodge City Comm. College Dodge City KS	dc3.edu
Garden City Comm. College Garden City KS	gobroncbusters.com
Hutchinson Comm. College Hutchinson KS	bluedragonsports.com
Pratt Comm. College Pratt KS	prattcc.edu
Seward County Comm. College Liberal KS	scccsaints.com

Q. Maryland Junior College Ath. Conf. -Region 20
mdjuco.org

Allegany College of Maryland Cumberland MD	allegany.edu
Anne Arundel Comm. College Severna Park MD	aacc.edu/athletics
Cecil College Northeast MD	cecil.edu
Chesapeake College Wye Mills MD	letsgoskipjacks.com
College of Southern Maryland La Plata MD	csmd.edu/athletics
Comm. College of Baltimore County Catonsville MD	ccbcmd.edu/athletic
Comm. College of Baltimore County Dundalk MD	ccbcmd.edu/dundalk
Comm. College of Baltimore County Essex MD	ccbcmd.edu/essex
Frederick Comm. College Frederick MD	athletics.frederick.edu

Garrett College	garrettcollege.edu
McHenry MD	
Hagerstown Comm. College	hagerstowncc.edu
Hagerstown MD	
Harford Comm. College	hagerstowncc.edu
Bel Air MD	
Montgomery College	montgomerycollege.edu
Germantown MD	
Prince George's Comm. College	pgccowls.com
Largo MD	

R. **Massachusetts Junior College Ath. Conf. -Region 21**

Bunker Hill Comm. College	bhcc.mass.edu/athletics
Boston MA	
Comm. College of Rhode Island	ccri.edu
Warwick RI	
Dean College	dean.edu
Franklin MA	
Holyoke Comm. College	hcc.edu
Holyoke MA	
Mass Bay Comm. College	massbay.edu
Wellesley Hills MA	
Massasoit Comm. College	massasoit.mass.edu
Brockton MA	
Northern Essex Comm. College	necc.mass.edu
Haverhill MA	
Quinsigamond Comm. College	www.qcc.edu
Worcester MA	
University of Connecticut at Avery Point	averypoint.uconn.edu
Groton CT	

S.   **Mid Hudson Conf.- Region 15** - mhcsports.org

Dutchess County Comm. College	sunydutchess.edu
Poughkeepsie NY	
Orange County Comm. College	sunyorange.edu
Middletown NY	
Rockland Comm. College	sunyrockland.edu
Sufferin NY	
Sullivan County Comm. College	sunysullivan.edu
Loch Sheldrake NY	
Ulster County Comm. College	sunyulster.edu
Stone Ridge NY	
Westchester Comm. College	sunywcc.edu
Valhalla NY	

T.   **NJCAA- Region 15** - region15athletics.com

ASA The College For Excellence	asa.edu
Brooklyn NY	
Borough of Manhattan Comm. College	www.bmcc.cuny.edu
New York NY	
Bronx Comm. College	www.bcc.cuny.edu
Bronx NY	
Globe Institute of Technology	globe.edu
New York NY	
Kingsborough Comm. College	kccathletics.com
Brooklyn NY	
Monroe College	monroecollege.edu
New Rochelle NY	
Nassau Comm. College	ncc.edu
Garden City NY	
Queensborough Comm. College	www.qcc.cuny.edu
Bayside NY	
Suffolk County Comm. College	sunysuffolk.edu
Selden NY	

U.   **Mid-State Ath. Conf.- Region 3** - njcaaregion3.org

Broome Comm. College	bcchornets.com
Binghamton NY	
Cayuga Comm. College	cayugaspartans.com
Auburn NY	
Corning Comm. College	redbaronsathletics.com
Corning NY	
Finger Lakes Comm. College	flccathletics.com
Canandaigua NY	
Jefferson Comm. College	cannoneerathletics.com
Watertown NY	
Onondaga Comm. College	sunyocc.edu
Syracuse NY	
Tompkins Cortland Comm. College	tc3.edu/panthers
Dryden NY	

V.   **Michigan Comm. College Ath. Assoc. -Region 12**
      mccaa.org

Ancilla Comm. College	ancilla.edu
Donaldson IN	
Delta College	delta.edu
Univ. Center MI	
Glen Oaks Comm. College	glenoaks.edu
Centreville MI	
Grand Rapids Comm. College	grcc.edu
Grand Rapids MI	
Henry Ford Comm. College	hfcc.edu
Dearborn MI	
Jackson College	jccmi.edu
Jackson MI	
Kalamazoo Valley Comm. College	kvcc.edu
Kalamazoo MI	

Kellogg Comm. College	kellogg.edu
Battle Creek MI	
Lake Michigan College	lakemichigancollege.edu
Benton Harbor MI	
Lansing Comm. College	lcc.edu
Lansing MI	
Macomb Comm. College	macomb.edu
Warren MI	
Mott Comm. College	ncc.edu
Flint MI	
Muskegon Comm. College	muskegoncc.edu
Muskegon MI	
St. Clair County Comm. College	sc4.edu
Huron MI	

W.   Minnesota College Ath. Conf.- Region 13
mcac.org

Anoka-Ramsey Comm. College	anokaramsey.edu
Coons Rapids MN	
Central Lakes College	www.clcmn.edu
Brainerd MN	
Century College	century.edu
White Bear MN	
Dakota County Technical College	goblueknights.com
Rosemont MN	
Fond du Lac Tribal & Comm. College	fdltcc.edu
Cloquet MN	
Hibbing Comm. College	hibbing.edu
Hibbing MN	
Itasca Comm. College	www.itascacc.edu
Grand Rapids MN	
Mesabi Range CTC	www.mesabirange.edu/athletics
Virginia MN	

Minnesota State Com. & Tech College	minnesota.edu
Fergus Falls MN	
Northland Comm. & Tech College	northlandcollege.edu
Thief River Falls MN	
Rainy River Comm. College	rainyriver.edu
International Falls MN	
Ridgewater College	ridgewater.edu
Willmar MN	
Riverland Comm. College	riverland.edu
Riverland MN	
Rochester Comm. and Tech College	rctcyellowjackets.com
Rochester MN	
St. Cloud Technical & Comm. College	sctcc.edu
St. Cloud MN	
Vermilion Comm. College	vcc.edu
Ely MN	
Western Wisconsin Tech	westerntc.edu
La Crosse WI	

X. **Mon-Dak Ath. Conf.- Region 13** - mondak.org

Bismarck State College	bismarckstate.edu
Bismarck ND	
Dakota College	dakotacollege.edu
Bottineau ND	
Dawson Comm. College	dawsonbucs.com
Glendive MT	
Lake Region State College	lrsc.edu
Devil's Lake ND	
Miles Comm. College	mccpioneers.com
Miles City MT	
Williston State College	willistonstate.edu
Williston ND	

Y. NJCAA Region 16

Cottey College Nevada MO	cottey.edu
Jefferson College Hillsboro MO	jeffco.edu
Metropolitan Comm. College Kansas City MO	mcckc.edu
Mineral Area College Park Hills MO	mineralarea.edu
North Central Missouri College Trenton MO	www.ncmissouri.edu
St. Charles Comm. College Cottleville MO	stchas.edu
St. Louis Comm. College St. Louis MO	archersathletics.com
Wentworth Military Academy Lexington MO	wma.edu/athletics

Z. NJCAA Region 23 Louisiana/Mississippi

Baton Rouge Comm. College Baton Rouge LA	mybrcc.edu
Coahoma Comm. College Clarksdale MS	coahomasports.com
Copiah-Lincoln Comm. College Wesson MS	colinathletics.com
Delgado Comm. College New Orleans LA	dcc.edu
East Central Comm. College Decatur MS	www.eccc.edu/athletics
East Mississippi Comm. College Scooba MS	athletics.eastms.edu

Hinds Comm. College
        Raymond MS

hindsec.edu

Holmes Comm. College
        Goodman MS

holmesathletics.com

Itawamba Comm. College
        Fulton MS

iccms.edu

Jones County Junior College
        Ellisville MS

jcjcathletics.com

Louisiana State University
        Eunice LA

lsue.edu

Mississippi Delta Comm. College
        Moorhead MS

msdelta.edu

Mississippi Gulf Coast Com. College
        Perkinston MS

mgccbulldogs.com

Northeast Mississippi Comm. College
        Booneville MS

nemccathletics.com

Northwest Mississippi Comm. College
        Senatobia MS

nwccrangers.com

Pearl River Comm. College
        Popularville MS

prcc.edu

Southwest Mississippi Comm. College
        Summit MS

smcc.edu

AA.   **Metro Ath. Conf. - Region 5**
       dcccd.edu

Brookhaven College
        Farmers Branch TX

brookhavencollege.edu

Cedar Valley College
        Lancaster TX

dcccd.edu

Eastfield College
        Mesquite TX

eastfieldcollege.com

Mountain View College
        Dallas TX

mvc.dcccd.edu

North Lake College   northlakescollege.edu
    Irving TX
Richland College   rlc.dcccd.edu
    Dallas TX

BB.   **North Texas Junior College Athletic Conf. - Region 5**
       njcaaregion5.com

Cisco College   www.cisco.edu
    Cisco TX
Grayson College   grayson.edu
    Dennison TX
Hill College   hillcollege.edu
    Hillsboro TX
McLennan Comm. College   mclennan.edu
    Waco TX
North Central Texas College   nctcathletics.com
    Gainesville TX
Ranger College   rangercollege.edu
    Ranger TX
Temple College   templejc.edu
    Temple TX
Vernon College   vernoncollege.edu
    Vernon TX
Weatherford College   wc.edu
    Weatherford TX

CC.   **Western Junior College Ath. Conf. - Region 5**
       njcaaregion5.com

Clarendon College   clarendoncollege.edu
    Clarendon TX
El Paso Comm. College   epcc.edu
    El Paso TX

Frank Phillips College   fpctx.edu
        Borger TX
Howard College   howardcollege.edu
        Big Spring TX
Luna Comm. College   luna.edu
        Las Vegas NM
Midland College   midland.edu
        Midland TX
New Mexico Junior College   nmjc.edu
        Hobbs NM
New Mexico Military Institute   nmmi.edu/athletics
        Roswell NM
Odessa College   odessa.edu
        Odessa TX
Western Texas College   wtc.edu
        Snyder TX

DD.   **Mountain Valley Ath. Conf.- Region 3**

SUNY Adirondack   sunyacc.edu
        Queensbury NY
Clinton Comm. College   clinton.edu/athletics
        Plattsburgh NY
Columbia-Greene Comm. College   cgcctwins.com
        Hudson NY
Fulton-Montgomery Comm. College   fmcc.edu/athletics
        Johnstown NY
Herkimer County Comm. College   herkimergenerals.com
        Herkimer NY
Hudson Valley Comm. College   hvcc.edu/athletics
        Troy NY
Mohawk Valley Comm. College   gomvhawks.com
        Utica NY
North Country Comm. College   nccc.edu/athletic
        Saranac Lake NY

Schenectady County Comm. College   sunysccc.edu
          Schenectady NY

EE.   **Scenic West Ath. Conf. -Region 18**
          scenicwestsports.com

College of East Utah   eastern.usu.edu
          Price UT
College of Southern Idaho   csi.edu
          Twin Falls ID
College of Southern Nevada   csn.edu
          Henderson NV
Colorado Northwestern Com. College   cncc.edu
          Rangley CO
College of Eastern Utah   ceu.edu
          Price UT
Northern Idaho College   nic.edu
          Coeur de Alene ID
Salt Lake Comm. College   slccbruins.com
          Salt Lake City UT
Western Nevada College   wnc.edu
          Carson City NV
Snow College   snow.edu
          Ephrain UT

FF.   **Ohio Comm. College Ath. Conf.- Region 12**
          occac.org

Cuyahoga Comm. College   tri-c.edu
          Parna OH
Lakeland Comm. College   lakelandcc.edu
          Kirtland OH
Lorain County Comm. College   lorainccc.edu
          Elyria OH

Owens Comm. College   owens.edu
        Perrysburg OH
Sinclair Comm. College   sinclair.edu
        Dayton OH

GG.   Western New York Ath. Conf.- Region 3

Alfred State College   alfredstateathletics.com
        Alfred NY
Erie Comm. College   ecc.edu/about
        Buffalo NY
Genesee Comm. College   genesee.edu/athletics
        Batavia NY
Jamestown Comm. College   sunyjcc.edu
        Jamestown NY
Mercyhurst University   mercyhurst.edu
        Mercyhurst PA
Monroe Comm. College   mcctribunes.com
        Rochester NY
Niagara County Comm. College   ncccathletics.com
        Sanborn NY

HH.   Southwest Junior College Conf. - Region 14
        njcaaregion14.com

Alvin Comm. College   alvincollege.edu
        Alvin TX
Angelina College   angelina.edu
        Lufkin TX
Blinn College   blinn.edu
        Brenham TX
Bossier Parish Comm. College   bpcc.edu
        Bossier City LA
Coastal Bend College   coastalbend.edu
        Beeville TX

Galveston College	www.gc.edu
Galveston TX	
Laredo Comm. College	laredo.edu
Laredo TX	
Navarro College	navarrocollege.edu
Corsicana TX	
Northeast Texas Comm. College	ntcc.edu
Mt. Pleasant TX	
Panola College	panola.edu
Carthage TX	
Paris Junior College	parisjc.edu
Paris TX	
San Jacinto College	sanjacsports.com
Houston TX	
Tyler Junior College	apacheathletics.com
Tyler TX	
Wharton County Junior College	wcjc.edu
Wharton TX	

II.   **Tennessee Comm. & Jun. College Ath. Assoc. - Region 7 -** tjccaa.com

Chattanooga State Comm. College	chattanoogastate.edu
Chattanooga TN	
Cleveland State Comm. College	clevelandstatecc.edu
Cleveland TN	
Columbia State Comm. College	columbiastate.edu
Columbia TN	
Dyersburg State Comm. College	dscc.edu
Dyersburg TN	
Jackson State Comm. College	jscc.edu
Jackson TN	
Motlow State Comm. College	mscc.edu
Lynchburg TN	

Roane State Comm. College   roanestate.edu
   Harriman TN
Southwest Tennessee Comm. College southwest.tn.edu
   Memphis TN
Volunteer State Comm. College volstate.edu
   Gallatin TN
Walters State Comm. College ws.edu
   Morristown TN

VI. Northwest Ath. Assoc. of Comm. Colleges (NWAACC) Baseball Colleges - nwaacc.org

CONFERENCE SCHOOL/CITY/ STATE	WEBSITE
Bellevue College Bellevue WA	bellevuecollege.edu
Big Bend Comm. College Moses Lake WA	bigbend.edu
Blue Mountain Comm. College Pendleton OR	bluecc.edu
Centralia College Centralia WA	centralia.edu/athletics
Chemeketa Comm. College Salem OR	chemeketa.edu
Clackamas Comm. College Oregon City OR	clackamas.edu/athletics
Clark College Vancouver WA	clarkpenguins.com
Columbia Basin College Pasco WA	columbiabasin.edu
Douglas College New Westminster BC	douglife.ca/dcroyalsathletics
Edmonds Comm. College Lynnwood WA	edcc.edu/athletics
Everett Comm. College Everett WA	everettcc.edu/athletics
Grays Harbor College Aberdeen WA	ghcathletics.com
Green River Comm. College Auburn WA	greenriver.edu
Lane Comm. College Eugene OR	lanetitans.net

Linn-Benton Comm. College Albany OR	linnbenton.edu/go/athletics
Lower Columbia College Longview WA	lccreddevils.com
Mt. Hood Comm. College Gresham OR	mhcc.edu/Athletics.aspx
Olympic College Bremerton WA	olympic.edu
Pierce College Lakewood WA	pierce.ctc.edu/athletics
Shoreline Comm. College Shoreline WA	shoreline.edu/athletics
Skagit Valley College Mount Vernon WA	skagit.edu
Southwestern Oregon Com. College Coos Bay OR	socc.edu/athletics
Spokane Comm. College Spokane WA	athletics.spokane.edu
Tacoma Comm. College Tacoma WA	tacomacc.edu/athletics
Treasure Valley Com. College Ontario OR	athletics.tvcc.cc
Walla Walla Comm. College Walla Walla WA	gowwcc.com
Wenatchee Valley College Wenatchee WA	www.wvc.edu
Yakima Valley Comm. College Yakima WA	goyaks.com

VII. California Comm. College Ath. Assoc. (CCCAA)
Baseball Colleges - cccaasports.org

CONFERENCE   WEBSITE
SCHOOL/CITY/ STATE

A. Bay Valley Conf.

Contra Costa College	contracosta.edu
San Pablo CA	
Laney College	laney.edu
Oakland CA	
Los Medanos College	losmedanos.edu/athletics
Pittsburg CA	
College of Marin	marin.edu
Kentfield CA	
Mendocino College	mendocino.edu
Ukiah CA	
Napa Valley College	napavalley.edu
Napa CA	
Solano College	solano.edu
Vallejo CA	
Yuba College	yccd.edu
Marysville CA	

B. Big 8 Conf.

American River College	arc.losrios.edu
Sacramento CA	
Cosumnes River College	crchawks.com
Sacramento CA	
Diablo Valley College	dvc.edu
Pleasant Hill CA	
Modesto Junior College	mjc.edu/athletics
Modesto CA	

161

Sacramento City College   scc.losrios.edu
    Sacramento CA
San Joaquin Delta College   deltacollege.edu
    Stockton CA
Santa Rosa Junior College   santarosa.edu
    Santa Rosa CA
Sierra College   sierracollege.edu
    Rocklin CA

C.   **Central Valley Conf.**

Fresno City College   fresnocitycollege.edu
    Fresno CA
Merced College   mccd.edu
    Merced CA
Porterville College   portervillecollege.edu
    Porterville CA
Reedley College   reedleycollege.edu
    Reedley CA
College of the Sequoias   cos.edu
    Visalia CA
Taft College   taftcollege.edu
    Taft CA
West Hills College   westhillsfalcons.com
    Coalinga CA

D.   **Coast Conf.**

Cañada College   canadacollege.edu
    Redwood City CA
Chabot College   chabotcollege.edu
    Haywood CA
Foothill College   foothill.edu
    Los Altos CA

Ohlone College	ohlone.edu
Fremont CA	
City College of San Francisco	ccsf.edu
San Francisco CA	
College of San Mateo	collegeofsanmateo.edu
San Mateo CA	
Skyline College	skylinecollege.edu
San Bruno	
Cabrillo College	cabrillo.edu
Aptos CA	
De Anza College	deanza.edu
Cupertino CA	
Gavilan College	gavilan.edu
Gilroy CA	
Hartnell College	hartnell.edu
Salinas CA	
Mission College	missioncollege.edu
Santa Clara CA	
Monterey Peninsula College	www.mpc.edu
Monterey CA	
West Valley College	westvalley.edu
Saratoga CA	

E.   **Foothill Conf.**

Antelope Valley College	gomarauders.avc.edu
Lancaster CA	
Barstow College	www.barstow.edu
Barstow CA	
Cerro Coso Community College	cerrocoso.edu
Ridgecrest CA	
Chaffey College	www.chaffey.edu
Cucamonga CA	
College of the Desert	collegeofthedesert.edu
Palm Desert CA	

Mt. San Jacinto College	msjc.edu
San Jacinto CA	
Rio Hondo College	riohondo.edu
Whittier CA	
San Bernardino Valley College	valleycollege.edu
San Bernardino CA	
Victor Valley College	vvc.edu
Victorville CA	

F.   **Golden Valley Conf.**

Butte College	butte.edu
Oroville CA	
Feather River College	athletics.frc.edu
Quincy CA	
Lassen College	lassencollege.edu
Susanville CA	
Shasta College	shastacollege.edu
Redding CA	
College of the Siskiyous	siskiyous.edu
Weed CA	

G.   **Orange Empire Conf.**

Cypress College	cypresscollege.edu
Cypress CA	
Fullerton College	fchornets.com
Fullerton CA	
Golden West College	gwathletics.com
Huntington Beach CA	
Irvine Valley College	ivc.edu
Irvine CA	
Orange Coast College	occpirateathletics.com
Costa Mesa CA	

Riverside City College
    Riverside CA
Santa Ana College
    Santa Ana CA

rcathletics.com

sacdons.com

H.   **Pacific Coast Ath. Conf.**

Grossmont College
    El Cajon CA
Imperial Valley College
    Imperial CA
Palomar College
    Marcos CA
San Diego City College
    San Diego CA
San Diego Mesa College
    San Diego CA
Southwestern College
    Chula Vista CA

www.grossmont.edu

imperial.edu

palomar.edu

sdcity.edu

sdmesa.edu

swccd.edu

I.   **South Coast Conf.**

Cerritos College
    Norwalk CA
East Los Angeles College
    Monterey Park CA
El Camino College
    Torrance CA
El Camino College - Compton
    Compton CA
Long Beach City College
    Long Beach CA
Los Angeles Harbor College
    Wilmington CA

cerritosfalcons.com

elac.edu

www.elcamino.edu

www.compton.edu

lbccvikings.com

lahc.edu

Mt San Antonio College	mtsac.edu
Walnut CA	
Pasadena City College	pasadena.edu
Pasadena CA	

J. **Western State Conf.**

Allan Hancock College	athletics.hancockcollege.edu
Santa Monica CA	
Cuesta College	cuesta.edu
San Luis Obispo CA	
Los Angeles Pierce College	piercecollege.edu
Woodland Hills CA	
Moorpark College	moorparkathletics.com
Moorpark CA	
Oxnard College	oxnardcollege.edu
Oxnard College CA	
Santa Barbara City College	sbcc.edu
Santa Barbara CA	
Ventura College	venturacollege.edu
Ventura CA	
Bakersfield College	gogades.com
Bakersfield CA	
College of the Canyons	canyons.edu
Santa Clara CA	
Citrus College	citruscollege.edu
Glendora CA	
Glendale Community College	glendale.edu
Glendale CA	
Los Angeles Valley College	lavc.edu
Valley Glenn CA	
Santa Monica College	smccorsairs.com
Santa Monica CA	
Los Angeles Mission College	lamission.edu
Sylmar CA	

West Los Angeles College   www.wlac.edu
Culver City CA

VIII.   United States Collegiate Ath. Assoc. (USCCAA)
Baseball Colleges/Universities - uscaa.org

CONFERENCE SCHOOL/CITY/ STATE	WEBSITE
Alice Lloyd College Pippa Pass KY	alc.edu
Alfred State College Alfred NY	alfredstateathletics.com
Andrews University Berrien Springs MI	aucardinals.com
The Apprentice School Newport News VA	gobuilders.com
Ave Maria University Ave Maria FL	avemariagyrenes.com
Briarcliffe College Bethpage NJ	briarcliffe.edu
Central Maine Community College Auburn ME	carlow.edu
Cincinnati Clermont College Batavia OH	ucclermont.edu
Clark State Community College Springfield OH	clarkstate.edu
Cleary University Ann Arbor MI	cleary.edu
Concordia College Alabama Selma AL	www.ccal.edu
University of Dallas Irving TX	udallasathletics.com
Eastern Maine Community College Bangor ME	gogoldeneagles.com
Iowa Wesleyan College Mt. Pleasant IA	iwc.edu

The King's College New York NY	tkc.edu
Lindenwood University-Belleville Belleville Il	lindenwoodlynx.com
University of Maine Presque Isle ME	umpi.edu
NHTI-Concord's Community College Concord NH	nhti.edu
Pennsylvania College of Technology Williamsport PA	pct.edu
Penn State University Beaver Monaca PA	br.psu.edu
Penn State University Brandywine Media PA	psubrandywineathletics.com
Penn State University- Fayette Lemont Furnace PA	fe.psu.edu
Penn State University McKeesport PA	athleticsga.com
Penn State University Hazleton PA	athletics.hn.psu.edu
Penn State University Mont Alto PA	psmontaltoathletics.com
Penn State University Schuylkill Haven PA	sl.psu.edu
Penn State University-Wilkes Barre Lehman PA	wb.psu.edu
Penn State University Worthington Dunmore PA	psuscrantonathletics.com
Penn State University York PA	psuyork.com
Robert Morris University Springfield Il	rmu.edu/athletics
Rochester College Rochester Hills MI	rochestercollegewarriors.com

College of St. Joseph's-Vermont Rutland VT	csj.edu
St. Joseph's College Brooklyn NY	sjcbears.com
Selma University Selma AL	selmauniversity.org
Southern Maine Community College Portland ME	smccme.edu
Southern Virginia University Buena Vista VA	svu.edu
SUNY Canton NY	canton.edu
SUNY College of Envir. Sc & For Syracuse NY	esc.edu
Vermont Technical College Williston VT	vtc.edu
Victory University Memphis TN	victory.edu
Washington Adventist University Takoma Park MD	wau.edu
Wentworth Military Academy Lexington MO	wma.edu
West Virginia U. In. of Technology Montgomery WV	wvutech.edu
The Williamson Free School Media PA	williamson.edu

IX. National Christian College Ath. Assoc. (NCCAA)
Baseball Colleges/Universities - thenccaa.org

CONFERENCE/ SCHOOL	WEBSITE	STATE
Arizona Christian University	arizonachristian.edu	AZ
Arlington Baptist College	arlingtonbaptistcollege.edu	TX
Azusa Pacific University	apu.edu	CA
Bethel College	bethelcollege.edu	IN
Bethesda University of California	buc.edu	CA
Bluefield College	bluefield.edu	VA
Cairn University	cairn.edu	PA
Campbellsville University	campbellsvilletigers.com	KY
Cedarville University	cedarville.edu	OH
Central Baptist College	cbc.edu	AR
Central Christian College	centralchristian.edu	NE
Chowan University	chowan.edu	NC
Clearwater Christian College	clearwater.edu	FL
Colorado Christian University	ccu.edu	CO
Covenant College	covenant.edu	GA
Crowley's Ridge College	crc.edu	AR
Dallas Baptist University	dbu.edu	TX
Dallas Christian College	dallas.edu	TX
Ecclesia College	ecollege.edu	AR
Fresno Pacific University	fresno.edu	CA
Geneva College	geneva.edu	NY
Grace College & Seminary	grace.edu	IN
Grace University	graceu.edu	NE
Greenville College	greenville.edu	IL
Hillsdale Free Will Baptist College	hc.edu	OK
Hiwassee College	hiwassee.edu	TN

Houghton College	houghton.edu	NY
Huntington University	huntington.edu	IN
Indiana Wesleyan University	indwes.edu	IN
Johnson University	johnsonu.edu/florida	FL
Johnson University	johnsonu.edu/tennessee	TN
Judson University	judsonu.edu	IN
Lancaster Bible College	lbc.edu	PA
Lee University	leeuniversity.edu	TN
Lincoln Christian University	lincolnchristian.edu	IL
Manhattan Christian College	mccks.edu	KS
Maranatha Baptist Bible College	mbu.edu/athletics	WI
McMurry University	mcm.edu	TX
Mid-America Christian University	macu.edu	OK
Mid-Continent University	midcontinent.edu	KY
Mississippi College	mc.edu	MS
Morthland College	morthland.org	IL
Mount Vernon Nazarene University	mvnu.edu	OH
North Central University	northcentral.edu	MN
North Greenville University	ngu.edu	SC
Oakland City University	oak.edu	IN
Ohio Christian University	ocutrailblazers.com	OH
Oklahoma Christian University	oc.edu	OK
Oklahoma Wesleyan University	okwu.edu	OK
Olivet Nazarene University	olivet.edu	IL
Palm Beach Atlantic University	pba.edu	FL
Point University	point.edu	GA
Shorter University	shorter.edu	GA
Simpson University	simpsonu.edu	CA
Southeastern University	seu.edu	FL
Southern Nazarene University	snu.edu	OK
Southern Wesleyan University	swu.edu	SC
Southwestern Assemblies of God University	sagu.edu	TX

Southwestern Christian University	swcu.edu	OK
Spring Arbor University	arbor.edu	MI
Taylor University	taylor.edu	IN
Tennessee Temple University	tntemple.edu	TN
The King's College	optonline.net	NY
The Master's College	masters.edu	CA
Toccoa Falls College	tfc.edu	GA
Trevecca Nazarene University	trevecca.edu	TN
Trinity Bible College	trinitybiblecollege.edu	ND
Trinity Christian College	trnty.edu	IN
Trinity International University	tiu.edu	IL
Union University	uu.edu	TN
University of Northwestern	unwsp.edu	MN
Valley Forge Christian College	valleyforge.edu	PA
Victory University	victory.edu	TN
York College	york.edu	NE

APPENDIX 2

NCAA Core Course Requirements

Division I: The following core courses in high school are required for each student-athlete who wants to compete, practice and/or receive a scholarship at an NCAA Division I school

    4 years of English

    3 years of math at the Algebra I level or higher

    2 years of natural or physical science (must have one lab course, if offered)

    1 year additional of English, math or natural/physical science

    2 years of social science, and

    4 years additional from above list or foreign language, philosophy or comparative religion.

A student-athlete must complete 10 core courses by their seventh semester of high school. Seven of the 10 core courses must be in English, math or science. These are the core courses which are used to calculate the GPA requirement under the NCAA eligibility rules. The GPA minimum requirement is calculated based on a standard four point scale, A-4, B-3, C-2, D-1.

Division II: The following core courses in high school are required for each student-athlete who wants to compete, practice and/or receive a scholarship at an NCAA Division II school

    3 years of English

    2 years of math at the Algebra I level or higher

    2 years of natural or physical science (must have one lab course, if offered)

    3 years additional of English, math or natural/physical science

1 year of social science, and

4 years additional from above list or foreign language, philosophy or comparative religion.

A student-athlete must complete 10 core courses by their seventh semester of high school. Seven of the 10 core courses must be in English, math or science. These are the core courses which are used to calculate the GPA requirement under the NCAA eligibility rules. The GPA minimum requirement is calculated based on a standard four point scale, A-4, B-3, C-2, D-1.[21]

---

[21] NCAApublications.com/productdownloads/CBSA.pdf.

APPENDIX 3

NCAA Sliding Scale Index

(Beginning August 1, 2016)

Core GPA		SAT	ACT
3.550 & above	400	37	
3.525		410	38
3.500		420	39
3.475		430	40
3.450		440	41
3.425		450	41
3.400		460	42
3.375		470	42
3.350		480	43
3.325		490	44
3.300		500	44
3.275		510	45
3.250		520	46
3.225		530	46
3.200		540	47
3.175		550	47
3.150		560	48
3.125		570	49
3.10 0		580	49
3.075		590	50
3.050		600	50
3.025		610	51
3.000		620	52
2.975		630	52
2.950		640	53
2.925		650	53
2.900		660	54

2.875	670	55
2.850	680	56
2.825	690	56
2.800	700	57
2.775	710	58
2.750	720	59
2.725	730	60
2.700	740	61
2.675	750	61
2.650	760	62
2.625	770	63
2.600	780	64
2.575	790	65
2.550	800	66
2.525	810	67
2.500	820	68
2.475	830	69
2.450	840	70
2.425	850	70
2.400	860	71
2.375	870	72
2.350	880	73
2.325	890	74
2.300	900	75
2.299	910	76
2.275	910	76
2.250	920	77
2.225	930	78
2.200	940	79
2.175	950	80
2.150	960	81
2.125	970	82
2.10	980	83
2.075	990	84
2.050	1000	85

2.025	1010	86
2.000	1020	86

NCAA Division I Sliding Scale to use prior to August 1, 2016 has a few modifications from the above listed scale. These changes include:

GPA	SAT	ACT
2.675	740-750	61
2.450	840-850	70
2.150	960	80
2.125	960	81
2.100	970	82
2.075	980	83
2.050	990	84
2.025	1000	85
2.000	1010	86

Division II: Does not use a sliding scale for eligibility. [22]

---

[22] NCAApublications.com/productdownloads/CBSA.pdf.

APPENDIX 4

Conference Index

College Conf. of IL & WI	NCAA - D3	109
Colonial Athletic Conf.	NCAA - DI	87
Colonial State Ath. Conf.	NCAA - D3	109
Commonwealth Coast	NCAA - D3	109
Commonwealth Conf.	NCAA - D3	110
Conference USA	NCAA - DI	88
Conference Carolina	NCAA - D2	97
Crossroads League	NAIA	125
East Coast Conference	NCAA - D2	97
Empire 8 Conference	NCAA - D3	110
Florida College Sys. Assoc.	NJCAA - Region 8	137
Foothill Conference	CCCAA	163
Freedom Conference	NCAA - D3	110
Garden State Ath. Conf	NJCAA - Region 19	139
Georgia Col. Ath. Assoc.	NJCAA - Region 17	141
Golden State Ath. Conf.	NAIA	126
Golden Valley Conference	CCCAA	164
Great Rivers Ath Conf.	NJCAA - Region 24	142
Great Lakes Valley Conf.	NCAA - D2	98
Great American Conf.	NCAA - D2	99
Great Lakes Intercol.	NCAA - D2	. 97
Great Plains Ath. Conf.	NAIA	126
Great Northeast	NCAA - D3	111
Great Northwest Ath. Conf.	NCAA - D2	98
Gulf Coast Athletic Conf.	NAIA	126
Gulf South Conference	NCAA - D2	99
Heart of America	NAIA	127
Heartland Collegiate	NCAA - D3	111
Heartland Conference	NCAA - D2	100
Horizon League	NCAA - DI	88
Illinois N4C Conf	NJCAA - Region 4	142
Illinois Skyway Conf.	NJCAA - Region 4	143
Iowa Comm. Col Ath. Conf.	NJCAA - Region 11	136
Iowa Inter. Ath. Conf.	NCAA - D3	111
Ivy League	NCAA - DI	88

NJCAA	Region 16	151
NJCAA	Region 19	140
NJCAA	Region 20	140
NJCAA	Region 23	151
NJCAA	Region 9	140
North Coast Athletic	NCAA - D3	116
North West Ath. Association	NWAACC	159
North Atlantic Conference	NCAA - D3	116
North Eastern Athletic	NCAA - D3	117
Northeast Conference	NCAA - DI	91
Northeast-10 Conference	NCAA - D2	101
Northern Athletic Conf.	NCAA - D3	117
Northern Sun Intercol.	NCAA - D2	102
Northwest Conference	NCAA - D3	117
Ohio Valley Conf.	NCAA - DI	91
Ohio Athletic Conf.	NCAA - D3	118
Ohio Comm. Col. Ath. Conf.	NJCAA - Region 12	155
Old Dominion Ath.	NCAA - D3	118
Orange Empire Conf.	CCCAA	164
Pacific Coast Ath. Conf.	CCCAA	165
Pacific West Conference	NCAA - D2	102
Pacific 12 Conf.	NCAA - DI	91
Patriot League	NCAA - DI	92
Peach Belt Conference	NCAA - D2	103
Penn State Ath Conf.	NCAA - D2	103
Presidents' Ath. Conf.	NCAA - D3	118
Red River Athletic Conf.	NAIA	129
Rocky Mountain Ath. Conf.	NCAA - D2	104
Scenic West Ath. Conf.	NJCAA - Region 18	155
Skyline Conference	NCAA - D3	119
Sooner Athletic Conf.	NAIA	129
South Coast Conference	CCCAA	165
South Atlantic Conf.	NCAA - D2	104
Southeastern Conf.	NCAA - DI	92
Southern Athletic Assoc.	NCAA - D3	119

Southernland Conf.	NCAA - D1	93
Southern Collegiate	NCAA - D3	120
Southern Conference	NCAA - DI	93
Southern Inter. Ath. Conf.	NCAA - D2	105
Southern State Ath. Conf.	NAIA	130
Southern CA Inter. Col.	NCAA - D3	120
Southland Conference	CAA - DI	93
Southwest Jun. Col. Conf.	NJCAA - Region 14	156
Southwestern Athletic Conf.	NCAA - DI	94
St. Louis Intercollegiate	NCAA - D3	120
St. Univ. of NY Athletic Conf.	NCAA - D3	121
Sunbelt Conference	NCAA - DI	94
Sunshine State Conf.	NCAA - D2	105
The Sun Conference	NAIA	130
The American Conference	NCAA - DI	83
The Summit League	NCAA - DI	94
TN Comm. Col. Ath. Assoc.	NJCAA - Region 7	157
University Athletic Assoc.	NCAA - D3	122
Upper Midwest Athletic	NCAA - D3	122
USA South Athletic	NCAA - D3	121
West Coast Conference	NCAA - DI	95
Western Jun. Col. Ath. Conf.	NJCAA - Region 5	153
Western Athletic	NCAA - D3	122
Western NY Ath. Conf.	NJCAA - Region 3	156
Western State Conference	CCCAA	166
Western Athletic Conf.	NCAA - DI	95
Wisconsin Intercollegiate	NCAA - D3	122
Wolverine Hoosier Conf.	NAIA	131
WV Inter Ath. Conf.	NCAA - D2	106

ABOUT THE AUTHORS

Richard O'Connor has been active in college level baseball for the past two decades as an advisor and founder/director of the *Silver Spring-Takoma Thunderbolts*, a collegiate summer wooden bat baseball team in Maryland. Richard is also a co-founder of the Cal Ripken Collegiate Baseball League. A former college player, Richard received an undergraduate degree from Boston University (A.B.) and graduate degrees from the University of Michigan (Masters of Regional Planning) and Cooley Law (J.D.) Richard has been a trial attorney for the past 30 year. A native of Wellesley, Massachusetts, he resides in Takoma Park, Maryland, with his wife. He has two sons, Patrick and Kevin, and a new grandson, Kellan.

David B. Stinson, a long-time youth baseball coach, is the current Director of Player Personnel and former General Manager of the *Silver Spring-Takoma Thunderbolts*. David received an undergraduate degree from the University of Maryland (B.S.) and a graduate degree from American University (J.D.). A former litigator for the U.S. Department of Justice, David is the creator and owner of *deadballbaseball.com*, a website dedicated to the lost ballparks of professional baseball. David resides with his wife in Silver Spring, Maryland. Visit him at *davidbstinsonauthor.com* or contact him at *huntingtonparkdbs@gmail.com*.